THE
STRATEGIC
PARTNERING
POCKETBOOK

D0864684

I Cubed Innovations Inc.

THE
STRATEGIC
PARTNERING
POCKETBOOK

BUILDING STRATEGIC
PARTNERSHIPS AND ALLIANCES

TONY LENDRUM
CARTOONS BY JOCK MACNEISH

The **McGraw·Hill** Companies

Sydney New York San Francisco Auckland
Bangkok Bogotá Caracas Hong Kong
Kuala Lumpur Lisbon London Madrid
Mexico City Milan New Delhi San Juan
Seoul Singapore Taipei Toronto

Information contained in this work has been obtained by McGraw-Hill from sources believed to be reliable. However, neither McGraw-Hill nor its authors guarantee the accuracy or completeness of any information published herein, and neither McGraw-Hill nor its authors shall be responsible for any errors, omissions or damages arising out of the use of this information. The work was published with the understanding that McGraw-Hill and its authors are supplying information but are not attempting to render engineering or other professional services. If such services are required, the assistance of an appropriate professional should be sought.

Text © 2004 Tony Lendrum
Illustrations and design © 2004 McGraw-Hill Australia Pty Ltd
Additional owners of copyright are acknowledged on the Acknowledgments page.

Apart from any fair dealing for the purposes of study, research, criticism or review, as permitted under the *Copyright Act*, no part may be reproduced by any process without written permission. Enquiries should be made to the publisher, marked for the attention of the Permissions Editor, at the address below.

Every effort has been made to trace and acknowledge copyright material. Should any infringement have occurred accidentally the authors and publishers tender their apologies.

Copying for educational purposes
Under the copying provisions of the *Copyright Act*, copies of parts of this book may be made by an educational institution. An agreement exists between the Copyright Agency Limited (CAL) and the relevant educational authority (Department of Education, university, TAFE, etc.) to pay a licence fee for such copying. It is not necessary to keep records of copying except where the relevant educational authority has undertaken to do so by arrangement with the Copyright Agency Limited.

For further information on the CAL licence agreements with educational institutions, contact the Copyright Agency Limited, Level 19, 157 Liverpool Street, Sydney NSW 2000. Where no such agreement exists, the copyright owner is entitled to claim payment in respect of any copies made.

Enquiries concerning copyright in McGraw-Hill publications should be directed to the Permissions Editor at the address below.

National Library of Australia Cataloguing-in-Publication data:

Lendrum, Tony
The strategic partnering pocketbook: building strategic partnerships and alliances.
Includes index.
ISBN 0 074 71403 1.
Strategic alliances (Business). 2. Partnership. 3. Organizational change. I. Title
658.042

Published in Australia by
McGraw-Hill Australia Pty Ltd
Level 2, 82 Waterloo Road, North Ryde NSW 2113
Acquisitions Editor: Eiko Bron
Production Editor: Rosemary McDonald
Editor: Ruth Matheson
Proofreader: Tim Learner
Indexer: Diane Harriman
Designer (cover and interior): Jan Schmoeger/Designpoint
Illustrator: Alan Laver, Shelly Communications
Cartoonist: Jock Macneish
Typeset in 9/12 pt ITC Stone Serif by Jan Schmoeger/Designpoint
Printed on 80 gsm woodfree by Pantech Limited, Hong Kong.

The **McGraw·Hill** Companies

Contents

The vision

Making our world a better place.

The definition—strategic partnering and alliancing

The cooperative development of successful, continuously improving, long-term, strategic relationships, based on mutual trust, world class/best practice, sustainable competitive advantage and benefits for all the partners; they are relationships that have a further separate and positive impact outside the partnership/alliance.

The way

- **Keep the faith**—in the guiding principles and values for the relationship.
- **Stay focused**—on the strategic drivers for the business and the value propositions for the relationship.
- **Enjoy the journey**—learn, have fun and celebrate success.

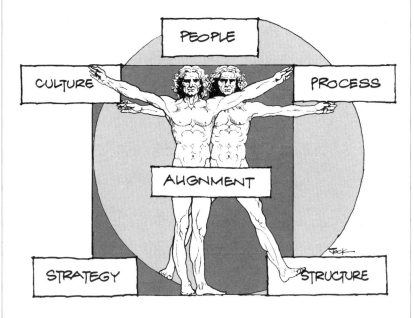

About Tony Lendrum
and Jock Macneish

Tony Lendrum is CEO and Head Coach, Trainer, Facilitator at Strategic Partnering Pty Ltd, a management consulting firm he formed in September 1994 to specifically work with organisations interested in pursuing the benefits of strategic partnering and alliance relationships. Tony's experience in partnering, alliancing and relationship management spans more than 20 years, 14 of which were spent with ICI, the global chemical company. An honours degree physical chemist by education, Tony has worked in many and various technical, sales, marketing, management, business development and manufacturing roles. This included two years in South Korea with responsibility for acquisitions, joint ventures and new business opportunities. He was also Operations Manager for one of ICI Australia's petrochemical plants in Sydney. Tony is also an experienced partnering and alliance manager. His first book *The Strategic Partnering Handbook*, now in its fourth edition, is widely used by small, medium and large organisations in the private and public sector as a practical guide to implementing high-performance, collaborative, long-term, strategic relationships.

Jock Macneish was born in Trinidad and went to school in Scotland. He studied architecture in London and in Melbourne and has worked in many parts of the world, including two years in Papua New Guinea. His work covers architecture, acoustic consultancy, illustrations and cartooning. One of Australia's best-known cartoonists, Jock is the coauthor of many successful books on teams and productivity in the workplace and now runs a company that creates images designed to carry ideas. He calls them 'Strategic Images'. He lives in Melbourne, and loves to draw cartoons. Some of the images in this Pocketbook were also developed in collaboration with Tony Richardson who has coauthored several books with Jock.

Preface

Strategic partnerships and alliances are about trust and transparency around common goals for mutual benefit. *The Strategic Partnering Pocketbook* has been written as an easy-to-read, ready reference for managing strategic partnering and alliance relationships.

The models, tools, applications, checklists and diagnostics in this Pocketbook are as relevant to the directors in the boardroom as they are to the employees at the 'coalface', shop floor and operating levels, as well as all the people in between. Having a common understanding, language and practice around relationship management, and in particular partnering and alliance relationships, is critical for success. This Pocketbook will assist in turning the rhetoric into reality, and provide some fun and laughs along the way.

Strategic partnerships and alliances are a logical response to the globalisation of markets, increasingly intense competition, the need for faster innovation based on continuous and breakthrough improvement, and the growing complexity of technology. Few organisations can go it alone these days and be successful. Past adversaries are quickly becoming collaborative colleagues. Confrontation is turning into cooperation, competition into collaboration, mistrust into transparency, and separate and often-conflicting strategies into a shared vision and common goals. However, the fact that these partner and alliance relationships are developed over time, not overnight, is often misunderstood.

Strategic partnerships and alliances have many benefits. For example,

- They are now regarded as a legitimate fourth growth option for business alongside organic growth, acquisitions/mergers and divestments.
- They provide a new and effective model for public/private sector engagement.
- They can apply downstream with customers, upstream with suppliers, in parallel with 'complementors', and to internal relationships.
- They are fun and enjoyable, generating higher levels of work satisfaction, providing greater opportunities for learning and growth, and improving the employability of the people involved.

- Practising organisations are fast becoming the 'employers of choice' for high calibre, professional, relationship managers.

The Strategic Partnering Handbook, fourth edition, by Tony Lendrum is the 'big brother' to this Pocketbook. The Handbook provides a valuable reference for those people wanting to understand the next level of detail. Further information is also available at the website www.partneringcommunity.com.

Acknowledgments

Over and above all the people who have inspired me to write this book my thanks must go to Jock Macneish. He has brought the words alive through his pictures. Without Jock, his creativity and challenging discussions this book would not be complete. To all the other champions, pioneers and provocateurs I have met over the years, this is also your book. My sincere thanks to you all.

Chapter 1

A short story to start with

SuperCat and SmartChem turn confrontation into cooperation

This was not one of Brian's better days. He was late after becoming lost on his way to a 'Business review and development workshop'. He was the co-facilitator for the workshop, which was being held with a very large customer called SmartChem. The prime objective of the workshop was to resurrect an almost terminal relationship which, all being well, should have been an example of best practice and a referral point for new business. Brian was a little nervous and shaken because through lack of concentration he had failed to indicate when changing lanes and had almost run himself and another car off the road, narrowly avoiding a major accident.

As if this wasn't bad enough, Brian learns on his arrival at the workshop venue that his roadside adversary was Bob, the new General Manager of Smart-Chem whom he had heard about but had not yet met. It was Bob who was the original instigator of the workshop idea. 'Perfect,' Brian thought, 'I've just pissed off the new boss of an already unhappy customer who needs only a touch more aggravation to send the 10-year relationship into oblivion.'

Brian is a Key Account Manager for SuperCat, a manufacturer of specialty catalysts and associated engineering services. SmartChem, one of SuperCat's largest customers for almost 10 years, uses these catalysts to manufacture and wholesale speciality chemicals and associated services to a wide range of industries. The catalysts allow SmartChem to produce finished products with very specific properties and functionality for which their customers pay high premiums. The engineering services division of SuperCat maintains the SmartChem plant and equipment in which the catalysts are used.

Although there were isolated examples of outstanding performance, normally involving special projects and particular people, the relationship was characterised by: adversarial and defensive behaviour; an overpromise and underdelivery mentality on product development; poor service levels; stockouts at critical times; occasional quality problems; high staff turnover; variable project performance; cost variations; price and margin pressure; communications issues; poor information sharing; duplication of activities; and overall a complete lack of trust between the companies. This was indeed a remarkable relationship, but for all the wrong reasons!

Although Brian had some thoughts as to why this had happened, it was still essentially a mystery to him. It wasn't all SuperCat's fault. Brian muttered under his breath, 'it takes at least two to tango'. SmartChem's own requirements were unclear. They didn't seem to know what they or their customers wanted and the little they did know was not told early enough to SuperCat for them to constructively contribute or come up easily with new ideas and improvements. Unless the workshop could produce some fundamental changes, this once anticipated 'jewel in the crown' relationship was going to be terminated in an unfriendly manner and buried in the graveyard of lost opportunities.

Katherine is Brian's counterpart at SmartChem. Brian with a technical background as an engineer and Katherine with a background in general business and finance complemented each other well in competencies, values and personality. Both knew that while many of the issues presented themselves as technical gaps and problems, these were just the symptoms. Technology itself, in most cases, was not the root cause of the difficulties between the companies. It was a whole range of relationship 'things' involving people, personalities, egos, poor communication, little information sharing, poor alignment of goals, no early warnings, low trust and a whole lot more.

Brian told Katherine about his 'road warrior' experience and that it was a speeding Bob he had nearly run off the road. Katherine's initial reading of Bob, although she had known him for only a short time, was that he was tough but fair, set high standards and had high expectations. 'You had better square it off with him now, as we don't want to be carrying any baggage into the workshop that could cause us grief later,' Katherine advised Brian. She was right. Brian fronted up to Bob with an extended hand in apology, 'Brian

Jones from SuperCat, Bob. I'm really sorry about what happened on the road this morning. It was my fault, no excuses.' To his surprise Bob not only accepted the apology but added, 'I thought about it afterwards, Brian, and to be honest I was going too fast, I was in too much of a hurry and I probably caught your blind spot at the wrong time. In the end no one was hurt and I think we both learnt a lesson or two.' As both men moved into the workshop Brian experienced a sense of relief. 'He sounds like a reasonable bloke—that's one crisis averted,' thought Brian.

What to do—where to from here?

As host and co-facilitator with Katherine, Brian was to make the opening presentation to the assembled group. The temptation was to go for the detail followed by the excuses. His technical people had given him a huge amount of data to support their case. This is the way they have always done it—confuse, frustrate and deny with detail. In light of the morning's events and the sight of 25 agitated people from engineering, maintenance, operations, procurement, sales and senior management—with two warring tribes all wanting answers, solutions and actions now—Brian felt compelled to try a different approach.

Noticing Brian was a little uneasy, Katherine whispered, 'When in doubt keep it simple. Tell them a story.' Brian thought about what happened on the road earlier and his 'near-death experience' with Bob. He took a deep breath and proceeded to tell the story of how he had become lost and late and the subsequent traffic altercation. 'This aligned nicely,' he told the group, 'with the lack of clear direction and objectives for our relationship, little early involvement in planning and forecasting and the subsequent blame and finger pointing from both organisations when things go wrong.'

Bob knew where Brian was heading too, and he liked the idea of a short story to avoid death by detail and confrontation. He was new to this industry—a marketing guy by trade, and not a 'techo'. He was not looking forward to an adversarial day full of acronyms and technical jargon that he didn't understand. 'I was speeding, in a hurry and in the middle of Brian's blind spot,' Bob said supportively. He then added, 'as it turns out we were coming to the same place, at the same time for the same reason. If we both had known this earlier we could have teamed up, with one driving and one navigating. The incident would have been averted and we could have shared some innovative ideas and thoughts for improvement along the way.'

Impressed by Bob's openness and the fact he had nothing to lose, Brian decided to say what had been on his mind for some time. 'It takes two to tango. With the benefit of hindsight both companies must do things differently. We must practise prevention rather than cure. That way we turn problems into opportunities.'

Brian heard a couple of 'snipers' off to the side mumble 'like that's breaking new ground, Einstein'. Brian made a mental note to 'keep a watchful eye on these two potential troublemakers'. 'There is no rocket science here,' Brain added. 'We prevent problems before they occur. To do that we have to talk and share information sooner rather than later—something we have not done in the past. We also have to ask: "How can we do things differently and better, rather than find reasons why we can't?"'

Brian continued, 'I think 99.9 per cent of people are decent, fair-minded and reasonable. So why is it that for most of us, for most of the time, we are at each other's throats? At the core I think we are two fundamentally competent and principled companies with aligned business drivers and objectives. We are doing some very important business together for ourselves, our customers, our shareholders and other stakeholders, including the environment and community at large. But we don't trust each other. We keep secrets, we tell lies and the relationship is full of unpleasant surprises. It seems to me that it should be the reverse. I don't know what the answer is, but I do know a solution exists. We as one team have to find it.'

'A colleague handed me a book a couple of weeks ago called *The Strategic Partnering Handbook*. It's all about strategic partnerships and alliances. It talks about a spectrum of relationship approaches from vendor to supplier through to partner relationships, understanding where your relationships are and where you would like them to be. We must make a fundamental improvement in this relationship in both approach taken and performance achieved. Otherwise I think the relationship should be terminated as neither company is benefiting. Both organisations can put their time, effort and money elsewhere to better use and for better returns. We have reached a point of no return—a crisis point from which a fundamental change has to take place. "We," and by that I mean all of us, working as one team, heading in one direction with common goals—we either make the relationship work or terminate it.'

At this point you could have heard a pin drop. This was passionate and provocative stuff, and just what the group needed to challenge their comfort zone. 'Brian is absolutely right,' added Bob unexpectedly. The silence was now deafening. Bob continued, 'I've read the book that Brian mentioned and it appears to me, as a newcomer to this relationship, that the two companies are predominantly combative and tribal in their behaviours and practices towards each other, and this is not sustainable. We must have an interdependent, long-term, strategic, collaborative, transparent and trusting relationship if we are both going to be successful into the future. To do that we have to change the current relationship approach and the performance levels achieved, or change the relationship participants.'

Instinctively Bob had confidence in both Brian and Katherine to take this forward one way or the other. Although particularly unhappy with the relationship, because of the critical nature of the products and services, they

were not readily changeable and in any event the current trouble
all of SuperCat's making. There was much internal work to be do
SmartChem. This SuperCat relationship initiative may well provide
benefits in assisting SmartChem's internal transformation process. Bob knew
he had to give this relationship every chance and was surprised and impressed
with Brian's honesty and approach. He said, 'Frankly I never used to be a
partnering or alliance person. I thought relationships were for family, friends
and pets. However some different and rewarding experiences over the last
few years have changed my mind. But partnerships and alliances need to be
done between the right people for the right reasons.'

As a vote of confidence he added, 'I trust Katherine and Brian to lead a team
and the process forward with whatever resources they feel necessary. I am
also happy to sponsor the process; however I will need to be kept informed of
progress and I will need proof of positive change quickly and a level of comfort
that it is sustainable. There will also need to be a structure and a roadmap to
this partnering thing to ensure that knowledge is transferred effectively and
that the relationship survives and thrives beyond the life of key people. And
lastly you will need to demonstrate that this relationship is delivering value
over the alternatives. If SuperCat cannot deliver our requirements, current
and future, then we have to find someone who can.'

'Nothing like an ultimatum to focus the mind on improvement,' Brian
pondered.

The language and the argument were compelling and on the surface and
in public all agreed this was a sensible way to go. Turning the language and
the concepts into practical reality would be more challenging. The rest of the
day was spent detailing the issues that were on everyone's mind and working
through the next steps. Brian and Katherine knew that the way forward was
not going to be easy. It was going to be a rollercoaster journey requiring
leadership, vision and commitment at all levels. But they were excited by the
opportunity and encouraged by the support from Bob.

The SuperCat and SmartChem story is *to be continued* throughout this
Pocketbook. Read on and see what challenges they face, the changes they
make, the successes they achieve, the lessons they learn and what may be
applicable to your own relationships.

Chapter 2

The 0 to 10 Relationship Management Matrix

YOU CAN'T BE ALL THINGS TO ALL PEOPLE...

Partnering and alliance relationships aren't for everyone

The three legitimate relationship categories

> 'Customers are the reason suppliers exist. If you don't have a customer you don't have a job or a business.'

Not all relationships are the same or need to be. You can't be all things to all people, but you can be the right things to the right people. It is not appropriate, nor does your organisation have the time and resources, to have every relationship as a strategic partnership or alliance. There are three legitimate relationship categories or segments (vendor, supplier and partner), each of which needs to be managed differently in terms of five key components: organisational *culture, strategy, structure, process* and *people.*

- *Vendor organisations* have:
  - a deal-making, cost-focused, protective culture (offensive and defensive)
  - a least-cost, lowest-priced based strategy
  - a traditional limited contact/selling supply structure

— a basic selling/transaction process, which is serviced by
— sales representatives, traders and other 'deal makers'.

- *Supplier organisations* have:
  — a customer-focused, continuous improvement, total-quality culture
  — a differentiated strategy based on cost or value or a combination of both
  — a multilevel selling structure
  — a complex selling and buying process, where the accounts are serviced by
  — account managers, good project managers or key account managers, depending on the size and quality of the relationship.

- *Partner organisations* have:
  — a highly flexible, empowering and innovative partnership culture
  — world-class or best-practice value-adding strategies
  — a team-based structure
  — a process of relationship management that is managed by
  — the partnering/alliance manager acting as coach to the self-managed partnering and alliance team(s).

Figure 2.1 on page 8 illustrates the three legitimate relationship categories or segments that are possible with customers and/or suppliers and the five components of each type of relationship. The further the relationship moves to the right of the scale, and when done well, the greater and more diverse the benefits will be.

The 11 types of relationships and the 11 different performance levels

There are 11 relationship types that are possible within each of the three relationship categories of vendor, supplier and partner. These are shown on the 0 to 10 Relationship Management Matrix (Fig. 2.2). As illustrated in Figure 2.2 on page 9, there are also 11 different performance levels that can be achieved (the *y*-axis or vertical axis), which are explained in Table 2.1 at the end of this chapter.

The Relationship Management Matrix is a universal matrix applying to any customer and supplier relationships that are internal or external to the organisation, any marketplace, public or private sector for any product or service category. All business relationships fit somewhere on the matrix. Relationships in the context of 0 to 10 relationship management are those human associations, connections or interactions—real or virtual—that have a goal or a purpose.

Question: *Where do your business relationships sit on the matrix?*

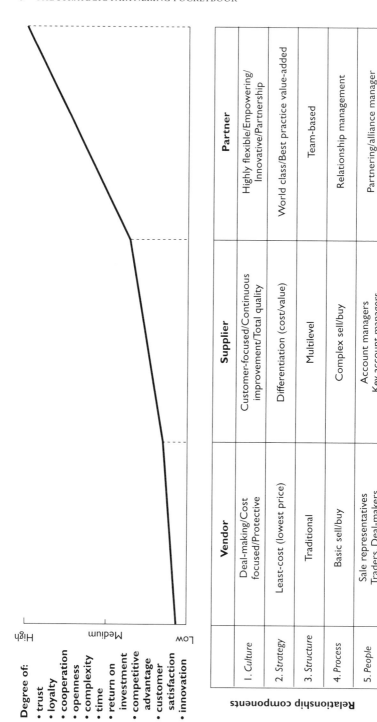

Degree of:
- trust
- loyalty
- cooperation
- openness
- complexity
- time
- return on investment
- competitive advantage
- customer satisfaction
- innovation

Relationship components	Vendor	Supplier	Partner
1. Culture	Deal-making/Cost focused/Protective	Customer-focused/Continuous improvement/Total quality	Highly flexible/Empowering/Innovative/Partnership
2. Strategy	Least-cost (lowest price)	Differentiation (cost/value)	World class/Best practice value-added
3. Structure	Traditional	Multilevel	Team-based
4. Process	Basic sell/buy	Complex sell/buy	Relationship management
5. People	Sale representatives Traders, Deal-makers	Account managers Key account managers	Partnering/alliance manager

Fig. 2.1 *Relationships between customers and suppliers and the five relationship components*

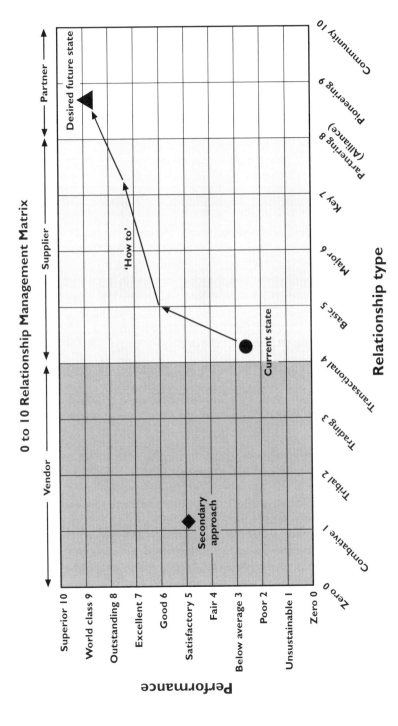

Fig. 2.2 *The 0 to 10 Relationship Management Matrix*

The six components of the 0 to 10 Relationship Management Matrix

The 0 to 10 Relationship Management Matrix has six components:

1. the 'relationship type'
2. the 'performance' achieved from the relationship
3. the 'current state' of the relationship
4. the 'desired future state' for the relationship
5. 'secondary approaches' applicable to the relationship
6. the 'how to' plan for bridging the gap between the 'current state' and the 'desired state'.

The relationship type

This is the horizontal or *x*-axis of the matrix. It represents the 11 legitimate relationship types split into the three categories or segments (vendor, supplier, partner). It is all about the practices, qualities, attributes, mindsets, attitudes and behaviours that are deployed in the relationship. These will be a function of the culture, strategy, structure, process and the people engaged in the relationship.

The performance achieved from the relationship

This is the vertical or *y*-axis of the matrix. It is about the results, effectiveness and performance, and the impact of the deployment of those practices, qualities, attributes, mindsets, attitudes and behaviours. The level of performance achieved in the relationship will be a function of six performance criteria:

1. *return on investment or financial success* (e.g. profitability, total cost improvements, revenues, overall value for money and other financial indicators)
2. *customer satisfaction* (e.g. quality, schedule and service levels, response times, business case or project completion outcomes, survey results, flexibility, responsiveness)
3. *sustainable competitive advantage* (e.g. market share/growth, customer/supplier loyalty/retention, referred business, bid rate success)
4. *world class/best practice implementation* (e.g. benchmarked efficiency, reliability, availability, work practices, implementation of systems, processes and procedures, the degree of operational excellence)
5. *innovation* (e.g. time to market, development cycle times, number and success rate of innovative ideas, continuous and breakthrough improvement)
6. *attitude* (e.g. behaviours, mindsets, trust levels, leadership, communications, openness, transparency, work practices, learning and growth opportunities, career development and promotional opportunities).

Each of these six performance criteria will be weighted differently for each relationship type.

The 'current state' and 'desired future state'

The *current state* of the relationship is a combination of how your organisation and the other organisation(s) currently approach the relationship. It is the prime current approach taken to the relationship. The *desired state* is the approach you, your organisation and/or the other organisations/stakeholders in the relationship would like to work towards in the medium to long term (e.g. three to five years). As Stephen Covey says, 'Begin with the end in mind.'[1]

Secondary approaches

Secondary approaches sometimes occur when the relationship is under pressure or stress or special projects/tasks have been or are being implemented with different approaches and/or varying performance levels from the 'prime' current state. The reality is that within complex, multisite, multibusiness, multipartner relationships there will most likely be a variety of secondary approaches—good, bad and indifferent—to be managed.

The 'how to' plan

The 'how to' plan involves the strategies, initiatives, actions and timelines by which the gap between the current state and the desired future state is bridged, and the secondary approaches are effectively managed.

In effectively developing partnering and alliance relationships it is the entire 0 to 10 Relationship Management Matrix that needs to be understood and managed. Understanding the 'current state' and the 'desired future state' of your relationships and implementing the 'how to' plan to bridge the gap is the key to effective relationship management.

For some relationships it is just a matter of improving performance and not moving to another relationship type—that is, doing what you are doing now but just doing it a whole lot better. This is not the case for partnering and alliance relationships however. In most instances they are a paradigm shift and not just a matter of doing the same things better. Going from 7 to 8 on the relationship scale or more generally from the vendor and supplier segments to the partner segment is not about incremental change or 'stretch target' improvement alone, reducing costs a further few dollars, improving customer service a notch, getting stock levels down a smidgen and products to market a few days earlier, or winning another percentage point of market share. Partnering and alliance relationships are about a fundamental change and breakthrough improvements in attitude, mindset, practice, performance and behaviour.

The definition of insanity: 'Doing the same things and expecting different results.'

In other words,

'If you always do what you have always done, then you will always get what you have always got!'

Understanding the relationship types and performance levels required, up and down the supply chain as well as internal to the organisation, and aligning the individual relationship strategies with the corporate strategy will be one of the secrets to your future success.

The 11 relationship types

The 11 possible relationship types in the 0 to 10 Relationship Management Matrix are explained below.

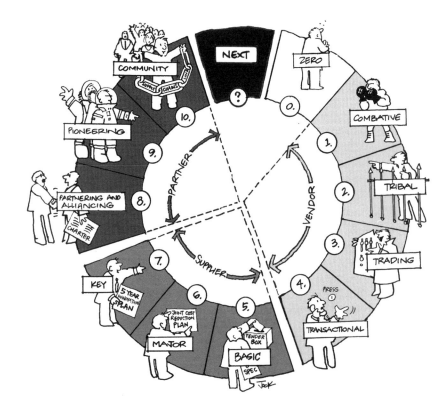

Type 0—Zero relationships

In a zero relationship the choice is made, deliberately and consciously, for good reason(s), not to have a relationship with the customer, supplier or competitor in question. It may also be a relationship that has been lost, which it is desired to regain or develop. In a 'zero' relationship, the parties' strategies, values, products and/or services are not aligned.

Type 1—Combative relationships

These are confrontational, adversarial, aggressive, coercive, uncooperative relationships based on mistrust, win/lose, master/slave, bullying, control/compliance mentality, arrogance, the need for secrecy and a short-term profit focus. They are often associated with hard-nosed, hard-dollar, tightly managed, detailed, one-sided contracts.

The partner from hell—it takes two to tango!

Type 2—Tribal relationships

These relationships are territorial, defensive, self-interest based, and protective of information, knowledge, skills, profits, margins, organisation, department, function, position or power base. They are parochial, often risk-adverse relationships with many internal and external demarcations, factions, organisational silos, little trust and a focus more on keeping secrets and apportioning blame than seeking win/win solutions for improvement.

Type 3—Trading relationships

These relationships live in a world of short-term opportunism, bargaining, bartering, 'horse-trading', little loyalty, low margins and little differentiation. The emphasis is on 'doing the deal' or retaining existing business, and getting or giving the order predominantly at the best or lowest price.

Type 4—Transactional relationships

These relationships do business predominantly over the counter (electronic or retail), over the telephone, by fax or over the Internet, with little or no negotiation involved. They are often arm's length, faceless, impersonal, systems or technology-based relationships.

Type 5—Basic relationships

These relationships are low impact, low profile, low priority, non-critical, non-core, independent, 'no frills', 'business as usual' relationships with a focus on the short to medium term and performance against budgets. The major focus is on price, basic quality and measured delivery of agreed requirements 'In Full On Time to A1 specification' (IFOTA1), often via contracts or service-level agreements, won through a tender or competitive bid process. There is little or no focus on and/or requirement for innovation or continuous improvement. Any improvements in products and services are either reactive or driven by general market trends.

Type 6—Major relationships

These relationships focus on total systems cost reductions, against agreed baselines, over and above IFOTA1 delivery of agreed requirements. There is a sharing of business goals, objectives, performance drivers/measures and other information (e.g. joint Strengths, Weaknesses, Opportunities, Threats analysis—or SWOT) for improvement. They are customer-focused, continuous improvement and total-quality based with a medium-term to long-term focus more on reducing or improving total costs than adding value.

Type 7—Key relationships

These are long-term and strategic relationships. They exploit synergies between customer and supplier, share strategy and other relevant information, minimise areas of conflict and implement high levels of innovation to both add value and reduce total costs. This is in addition to conforming to a complex set of agreed requirements IFOTA1. Both customer(s) and supplier(s) in the relationship provide expertise over and above the products and services given or received. They are independent, enlightened self-interested relationships, and based on long-term, win/win outcomes for all parties.

Type 8—Partnering and alliancing relationships

'Partnering' or 'alliance' relationships, as well as having all the characteristics and qualities of a Type 7 'key' relationship, are above all things about mutual trust. This is a trust based on competence, character, interdependence, honesty and integrity in working together, in good faith, as individuals and teams, to achieve a shared vision and common goals/strategies for mutual benefit. These collaborative, cooperative relationships live in a world of transparency, seamless boundaries, frictionless commerce, team-based responsibility and accountability, performance-based remuneration, shared risk/reward, joint benchmarking, absence of tenders or competitive bidding in the traditional sense, and leveraging core competencies around a broad balanced scorecard of performance measures.

There is a shared governance of the relationship by joint leadership, management and/or operational teams who hold themselves mutually accountable for the wellbeing and success of the relationship. Partnering and alliance relationships are not only strategic, they are also seen as critical to the long-term wellbeing and success of the partners. They are benchmarks and role models for other high-performance relationships.

Type 9—Pioneering relationships

These relationships capture those paradigm shifters and pioneers daring to seek new relationship boundaries and break old rules. These are brave, bold and different relationships. Breakthrough thinking coupled with intelligent risk taking is encouraged, delivering both continuous and breakthrough improvement. Sometimes called virtual relationships, clusters or consortia networks, they are based on the same principles and concepts as Type 8 'partnering' relationships, but are at the next level of complexity and ambiguity. Co-producer, global relationships, co-ownership of assets, equity share arrangements, shared intellectual property via the relationship, virtual companies, advanced multipartner alliances, complex public/private sector relationships and no dispute relationships are just some examples of the activities that can be involved.

Type 10—Community relationships

'Community' relationships are reserved for the extended enterprise, extended customer/supplier networks and integrated supply chains that are starting to be seen in the airlines, operations and maintenance, computers and communications, the Internet, entertainment, emergency services and leisure sectors. They share a common 'sense of community' and working democracy, jointly benchmarking, pooling and sharing resources across the community. Linked by an interconnected and shared destiny, the community is 'legacy building', delivering sustainable triple-bottom-line benefits (business, social and environmental) for the common good.

The same principles, concepts and practices that apply to Type 8 'partnering' or 'alliance' relationships are now extended up and down complex supply and value chains. The relationship is seen as part of an extended enterprise, value chain or integrated supply chain relationship.

The 11 performance levels

Table 2.1 describes the 11 performance levels that are achievable in the 0 to 10 Relationship Management Matrix (refer Fig. 2.2).

Table 2.1 *The performance levels*

Performance level	Description
0—Zero	This is normally the starting point for the relationship. No results have as yet been achieved. The relationship may still be in the planning phase or the planning phase has been completed but the implementation is yet to start and/or deliver results
1—Unsustainable	The relationship has just started or almost finished; it is on the verge of collapse. Either way it cannot continue for long at these performance levels. Significant change is required for improvement or an exit strategy needs to be developed and implemented. The relationship cannot be sustained at current performance levels opposite the expectations or requirements. This may be a function of both internal and external factors
2—Poor	Relationship performance is well below expectations (i.e. miserable). This could be a function of early days of the relationship, few results yet achieved, unprofitable and/or uncompetitive performance levels against forecast or non-forecast expectations/requirements
3—Below average	Performance is ordinary and at most times is unacceptable as determined against an agreed average benchmark(s) or target(s). It is a point of concern or it may be early days with improvements to come. Either way the relationship is yet to deliver acceptable results. Results are delivering low service levels, product quality, profitability and/or growth, or are below breakeven point, budget and/or forecast
4—Fair	This is a 'just OK or barely OK' result against expectations/requirements. There are no pleasant surprises. It is unlikely to deliver profitable growth or sustainable competitive advantage. It is at or a little better than a breakeven result. This is mediocrity
5—Satisfactory	This is an average, baseline result against requirements/expectations. It is the midpoint, or business as usual, or nothing special. There may be little or no excitement. This performance level is often a position of change

(continued on page 20)

Table 2.1 *The performance levels (cont.)*

Performance level	Description
6—Good	You are satisfied. It is a good solid result against expectations/requirements, ideally with opportunities for improvement. There is conformance to requirements based on stretch targets. It is the first point of real acceptability on the results scale. Profitable and/or differentiated results opposite the competition are being achieved
7—Excellent	Wow! Great! Excellent! The results are hard and soft. There is sustainable competitive advantage and/or profitable growth gained. There is room for improvement only if appropriate. These are often better than expected results achieved against expectations and requirements
8—Outstanding	This is knock your socks off, 'stand out', 'best in class' performance/results. You are delighted with the current performance/outcomes against expectations/requirements. There are benchmarked (internal and/or external) competitive and sustainable results. This is a very acceptable goal for most relationships
9—World class	This is best-in-class and/or world class performance/results and you can prove it as benchmarked against appropriate Key Performance Indicators (KPIs). The relationship is used as a benchmark, role model and centre of excellence. The relationship has a positive ripple effect on others, and has a self-sustaining momentum. There is significant competitive advantage and/or profitable growth gained. You may need to focus on improving the relationship type or resetting the performance bar
10—Superior	This is best of the best. It is a rarity. This is as good as it gets in terms of performance, and is the ultimate performance goal for any relationship type. It is often more of a target and aspiration than a reality, as it is almost beyond measurement. The ultimate in competitive advantage, these performance results set the benchmarks for others to follow. Beware of diminishing returns to get there

The levers for change

The 0 to 10 Relationship Management Matrix is both effective and simple. Its universal application makes it one of the most powerful business tools for analysing where you are now and where you want to be in the future in terms of your relationships with your customers and suppliers. In the following chapters, the nature of partnering and alliance relationships is explored further. Also discussed is how culture, strategy, structure, process and people can be used as levers for change in moving from the current state to the desired future state for the relationship.

Chapter 3

Getting started

Don't get 'hung up' on labels

Call them what you like—partnering relationships, strategic partnerships, strategic alliances, alliance partnering relationships, alliance contracting or relationship contracting. It doesn't matter. What is important is that all the partners have a clear and common understanding of what is meant by these relationships, with a common language and passion about the practices, behaviours, attitudes, mindsets and performance levels required.

Many organisations find the language, principles and concepts of partnering and alliancing compelling, but have great difficulty 'walking the talk' into effective practice. Many so-called partnerships and alliances are nothing more than glorified, conventional, contractual relationships with a twist of cooperative rhetoric. Signing off on the relationship charter is next to useless if the executive teams do not support it and the details are not delivered by an informed, competent, committed and empowered workforce.

Table 3.1 *The components of the strategic partnership definition*

Part of definition	What this means
1. **Cooperative development**	This is a cooperative, collaborative, trustworthy development based on shared vision, common goals and guiding principles for which individuals and joint leadership and management teams hold themselves mutually accountable. Involved will be fair-minded and reasonable people acting in good faith
2. **Successful**	As measured against agreed Key Performance Indicators (KPIs), leading and lagging, hard and soft indicators, and associated KPI targets normally in the form of a balanced scorecard or performance scorecard for the relationship
3. **Continuously improving**	Based on incremental as well as step-change, breakthrough innovation at all levels of the relationship
4. **Long-term**	This is performance-based and outcomes-focused, and linked to extended-term arrangements, evergreen or 'life of ...' relationships
5. **Strategic**	The relationship and supporting value propositions are critical to the wellbeing of all the partners with a high degree of interdependence in that all partners have something fundamental to lose should the relationship breakdown or something fundamental to gain from its success
6. **Mutual trust**	Based on the competence and the character of the individuals and organisations working together in good faith for common goals in an environment of open, honest, transparent and timely communication and information sharing
7. **World class/ best practice**	Developed, implemented, measured and jointly benchmarked (internal or external) for improvement and mutual benefit
8. **Sustainable competitive advantage**	Generating sustainable value for the customer beyond the cost of creating it, greater than the price the customer is prepared to pay for it and which is superior to the competition
9. **Benefits for all the partners**	Based on a win/win relationship where both the risks and the benefits are shared and where an open, transparent, gain/pain share, risk/reward model, with incentives, is in place linking performance, measurement, attitudes, remuneration, profitable growth and sustainable competitive advantage
10. **Separate and positive impact**	The relationship is used as a role model, benchmark or centre of excellence and learning for other customer/ supplier relationships, or as a vehicle for internal transformation

What is a strategic partnership?

A strategic partnership or alliance can be defined as:

> 'The cooperative development of successful, continuously improving, long-term, strategic relationships, based on mutual trust, world class/best practice, sustainable competitive advantage and benefits for all the partners; they are relationships that have a further separate and positive impact outside the partnership/alliance.'

This definition has 10 key components, which are described in Table 3.1.

If parts of this definition do not suit your particular strategic partnership or alliance, then modify the definition to suit. However, irrespective of the definition developed, ensure there is common agreement on its makeup and a common understanding of its meaning. You need to ask:

Question: Does the definition pass the 'handshake' test? Does it provide the basis for a moral agreement between the partners, and not purely a contractual or legal agreement?

Exercise: How do your relationships measure up?

How do your relationships measure up against the 'strategic partnership' definition? Complete the checklist in Table 3.2, and give each part of the definition a score out of 10 as it applies to your most important relationships. Then think about the high and low points and what can be done to improve your relationships.

Table 3.2 Definition checklist for your strategic partnerships

Part of definition	Level of achievement in your customer/supplier relationships (score out of 10)
1. Cooperative development	
2. Successful	
3. Continuously improving	
4. Long term	
5. Strategic	
6. Mutual trust	
7. World class/best practice	
8. Sustainable competitive advantage	
9. Benefits for all the partners	
10. Separate and positive impact	
Total score out of 100	

Reality check: If you scored greater than 8 out of 10 in all categories you are doing well.

SmartChem and SuperCat ... continued

Let's see how SmartChem and SuperCat scored on the checklist (see Table 3.3).

Table 3.3 *Definition checklist for SmartChem and SuperCat*

Part of definition		Level of achievement in SmartChem/SuperCat relationship (score out of 10 and comments)	
1.	Cooperative development	3	On special projects only. No shared relationship strategy or joint governance approach
2.	Successful	3	Little success by all measures. Poor KPIs in place, too basic
3.	Continuously improving	2	Very little, normally reactive not proactive to improvement
4.	Long term	1	Not performance based and threat of disengagement if no change
5.	Strategic	3	No clear value propositions or understanding of each other's underlying strategies
6.	Mutual trust	0	None, and this is problem number 1
7.	World class/best practice	4	Some good things done but inconsistent and no plan
8.	Sustainable competitive advantage	2	Relationship a poor reference point for profitable growth and value creation
9.	Benefits for all the partners	1	Seen as one-sided, win/lose or lose/lose—not win/win
10.	Separate and positive impact	1	Seen as a 'lemon' relationship
	Total score out of 100	**20**	**Very ordinary!**

This simple exercise was a real eye-opener for everyone. They didn't realise how far they had to go for the relationship to be a demonstrable and sustainable success, but it was only early days and this was the first step on the new journey. One person on the core team questioned both companies' willingness and capability to do it, but after discussion it was jointly agreed that the benefits were worth the effort of a good up-front strategic review and cost/benefit analysis.

Strategic versus project partnering: Is there a difference?

Project partnering and alliancing is based on the same principles and many of the same practices, processes and tools as a strategic partnership. However it differs in scope and timeframe. A project-based relationship is often linked to a narrower strategic focus, operational focus, project scope or inten (e.g. the building of a hospital, major road, rail link, tunnel, manufacturing plant upgrades, and other capital and infrastructure projects). Organisations often use project partnerships or alliances, either as project bundles or a series of longer term interrelated projects, as a stepping stone to, or fundamental building blocks for, a strategic partnership or alliance.

Why pursue strategic partnerships over other legitimate relationships?

In some situations, there are good reasons for choosing a strategic partnering approach. These reasons can include:

- There are significant and compelling 'value propositions' behind the formation of the relationship or project.
- There is an unclear, unpredictable risk profile for the project(s) or relationship (i.e. many unknowns/variables requiring flexibility in approach, practices and behaviours).
- Risk is to be shared and not transferred among the partners.
- The relationship/project scope is not well defined or it is open-ended.
- The relationship is long term and of critical importance (e.g. for the life of the asset).
- High levels of innovation are required, with both incremental and breakthrough improvement.
- Total openness, honesty and transparency are required of the relationship.
- There are critical time/schedule deadlines to meet.
- There are unprecedented or challenging stretch targets on safety, quality or cost.
- There are significant community or environmental issues that require broad partner and stakeholder ownership, commitment, communication, consultation, engagement and involvement.
- The strategic value and commercial value is high, requiring a high degree of interdependence between the organisations (e.g. technology development, critical and/or ongoing operational activities or innovative financial engineering models are required).
- Core competencies between partner organisations need to be leveraged.
- The changing political environment requires committed, interdependent partners.

SmartChem and SuperCat ... *continued*

Virtually all of the above reasons for pursuing a strategic partnership applied to the SmartChem and SuperCat relationship. They looked like they were perfect candidates for a strategic partnership or alliance—so where to from here?

What are the benefits of working together?

Both customers and suppliers can achieve a range of benefits from a strategic partnership or alliance.

Customer benefits

Customer benefits can include:

- improved quality, fewer rejects, less waste
- lower operational costs
- reduced inspection time
- dramatically reduced customer complaints due to non-conformances
- lower prices in real terms (i.e. reduced total cost)
- superior performance or effect at lower, equivalent (or even higher) prices (i.e. greater value for money)
- improved productivity/efficiencies/process stability
- shorter lead times
- improved reliability, flexibility and dependability of supply
- improved cash flows and reduced working capital costs
- lower inventory and cycle times
- reduced product/service development time
- improved skills
- joint training and skills development
- fewer hassles and less frustration
- more time and resources available for downstream customers
- increased margins (i.e. increased total value) and profitability
- improved communication and people relationships
- increase in market share
- aggregate purchasing
- supplier-managed inventories
- improved/extended range of products and services
- early supplier involvement in product/service development
- elimination of waste associated with tenders, annual auctions and multiple suppliers
- elimination of litigation and adversarial confrontation
- improved development cycle times
- improved time to market
- joint planning and strategy development
- reduced capital and operational expenditure
- improved safety performance
- higher value, structured financing
- simplification and/or integration of networks, processes and systems
- leveraging off the global strength, brand and market knowledge of the partner(s)

- influencing partner product/service development activities
- full and effective engagement of resources
- incentives aligned with performance and financial success
- reduced or improved risk profile
- common or aligned systems and processes
- improved work practices, mindsets and behaviours.

Supplier benefits

Supplier benefits can include:

- larger volumes of products and services (domestic and/or export)
- longer term stability of supply
- greater stability of forecasts
- improved production efficiencies/cycle times
- higher quality or lower operational costs
- lower costs in real terms
- fewer hassles and less frustration
- improved skills from joint training
- increased margins and profitability
- fewer customer complaints/less waste
- improved communication and people relationships (internal and external)
- price premium over the competition (i.e. greater value for money)
- achievement of preferred supplier/preferred relationship status
- increased market share and access to new markets
- the partnership becomes a benchmark for other customer/supplier relationships
- greater responsiveness and flexibility in fulfilling customer expectations and resolving customer complaints
- improved rate of product/service development, development cycle times
- improved logistics and delivery systems
- greater integration of activities between divisions/departments
- fewer process steps and less complexity
- early involvement in product or service development
- scrapping of the dreaded tender system
- elimination of litigation and adversarial confrontation
- cross-company secondments
- greater transparency and openness
- improved safety performance
- reduced capital and operational expenditure
- co-location of people and assets
- people exchange programs
- greater levels of innovation

- reduced or improved risk profile
- improved project completion
- improved customer/supplier retention/loyalty
- greater levels of referred business.

The RAD analysis—a relationship 'health check'

A relationship alignment diagnostic (RAD) analysis examines your alignment with your partner organisation's approach to the relationship and the desired performance levels. It is a relationship 'health check'.

Exercise: Where do you want this relationship to be?

You need to answer three questions and place the number of each question at the appropriate point on the 0 to 10 Relationship Management Matrix (refer Fig. 2.2). (As a guide, the SmartChem and SuperCat RAD analysis is shown in Fig. 3.1.) The three questions to ask are:

1. How do 'we' currently approach this relationship (i.e. the relationship approach taken and the performance level achieved by our organisation)?
2. How do 'they' currently approach this relationship (i.e. your perception of the relationship approach taken and the performance level achieved by the other organisation in the relationship)?
3. What is 'our' desired future approach to this relationship?

For completeness have your partner(s) in the relationship do the same from their perspective and compare the results.

There is a particularly effective crosscheck with the RAD. Your question 1 and 2 is the other organisation's question 2 and 1 respectively. Cross-referencing the RAD responses to understand the degree of alignment or misalignment in thinking and approach is always a very enlightening exercise.

SmartChem and SuperCat ... continued

The core team and a representative mix of people from both organisations completed the RAD analysis. It was done initially as two separate SmartChem and SuperCat groups and the results combined (see Fig. 3.1). A joint discussion then took place to analyse why the numbers were where they were.

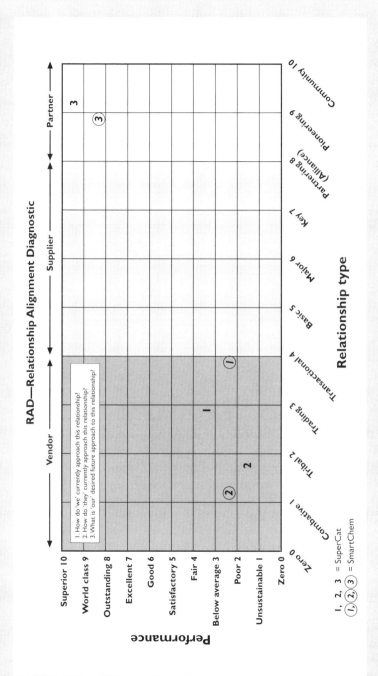

Fig. 3.1 *The RAD analysis: a relationship health check*

The RAD results were enlightening and confirmed what Brian and Bob had said at the workshop—that is, the perception and reality, and the behaviours and practices, from both organisations were primarily in the vendor segment, representing combative, tribal, trading and transactional behaviour delivering performance outcomes to less than satisfactory levels. It showed in stark and graphic terms that the current state of the relationship was not sustainable in the long term and certainly a long way from where both organisations wanted to be. A focused strategy led by committed people was required to bridge the gap between the current state and the desired future state.

From the joint discussions of each organisation's separate views (i.e. questions 1, 2 and 3), a combined 'current state' and 'desired future state' were agreed to (see Fig. 3.2). This enabled the team to begin their journey with the end in mind. From there they acknowledged they couldn't get to the desired state in one step and agreed to a 'three horizon approach' over two years to achieve their goals: Horizon 1 (six months); Horizon 2 (nine months); and Horizon 3 (nine months).

It was also observed that there were a number of secondary approaches that had taken place. The first was a particularly nasty incident where, through poor forecasting from SmartChem and poor stock management from SuperCat, a stockout of critically important products had occurred affecting SmartChem's largest customers. Both sides went for the contracts and the lawyers, and eventually SmartChem won a handsome out-of-court settlement that covered costs but did little for their image or brand in the marketplace (i.e. a combative/satisfactory secondary approach for SmartChem). This only reinforced the win/lose, combative unsustainable approach for SuperCat. The reality was it was a lose/lose for everyone.

The other two secondary approaches that were observed involved two special projects with differing levels of risk and clarity of scope, time deadlines, and

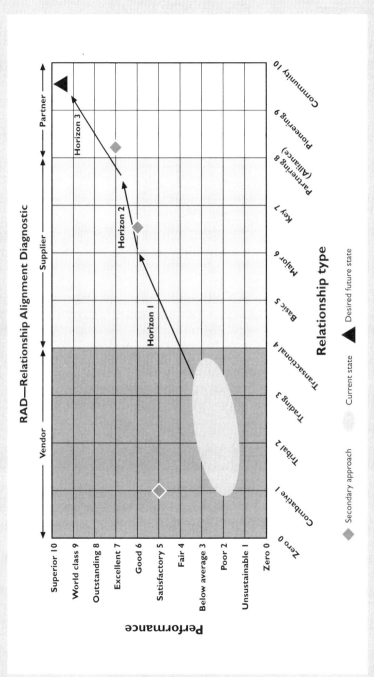

Fig. 3.2 *SmartChem and SuperCat's 'three horizon approach'*

environmental and community impact. The less critical project was delivered IFOTAI as required, with slightly better than expected cost management (i.e. a good result). The other was a high-risk project with critical time deadlines, a significant environmental and community impact, and a high probability of a cost blowout. The result achieved was outstanding and genuinely collaborative in approach, which was fundamentally different from the standard way the two organisations did business together. This was great news, and gave the core team confidence that Horizons 1, 2 and 3 could be achieved. They had demonstrated on a smaller scale project that they could behave and perform differently from the norm.

Analysing the top supporting relationships

It is also beneficial to do a RAD analysis on all the key supporting relationships (both internal and external) that will help you achieve your desired partnering relationship.

Exercise: Analyse your key supporting relationships

List and number your most important supporting relationships. Identify the current state of each of the relationships on the 0 to 10 Relationship Management Matrix and the desired future state. Formulate a strategy around bridging the gaps between the current and desired future states.

SmartChem and SuperCat ... continued

Brian and Katherine thought it would be a good idea to analyse the top (internal and external) supporting relationships to the SmartChem/SuperCat relationship. They were all a critical part of the value and supply chain that made the relationship a success or failure. The analysis (see Table 3.4) suggested that most of the current relationship states were not where they needed to be. Action plans were needed to improve the relationships.

Figure 3.3 shows the analysis of these top nine supporting relationships on the 0 to 10 Relationship Management Matrix. (Each relationship number is the same as the number in Table 3.4.) The number in italics indicates the current state of that particular relationship, while the number in bold indicates the desired future state (e.g. the No. 1 relationship of SmartChem and the Tank Cleaning Company is currently tribal and the desired future state is a 'zero' relationship).

Table 3.4 *Analysis of top supporting relationships*

	Relationship between	Comment
1.	SmartChem and Tank Cleaning Company	New service provider required. Current performance levels not sustainable
2.	SuperCat (Catalysts Division) and Number 1 raw materials supplier	Long-term strategic partnership required
3.	SuperCat (Catalysts Division) and SuperCat (Engineering Services)	Very defensive relationship with many demarcations; needs fundamental change
4.	SuperCat (Engineering Services) and SmartChem (Projects Department)	Good intent but poor delivery. Early planning and involvement with shared risk and reward needed
5.	SuperCat (Engineering Services) and Number 1 preferred construction company	Currently very 'arm's length' and very prescriptive. Approach and performance levels need to change
6.	SmartChem (Commercial Team) and SuperCat (Commercial Team)	Classic trading 'deal' vendor mentality; have to change to partner mentality
7.	SuperCat and freight company	Better performance with a planned cost improvement focus required
8.	SmartChem (Sales, Marketing, Research and Development) and SuperCat (Product Development and Operations)	More open communication, integrated Research and Development roadmap, teamwork and transparency required for maximum innovation
9.	SuperCat (Sales) and SuperCat (Production)	Currently a combative and adversarial relationship. Must develop trust, share all relevant information and significantly improve communications

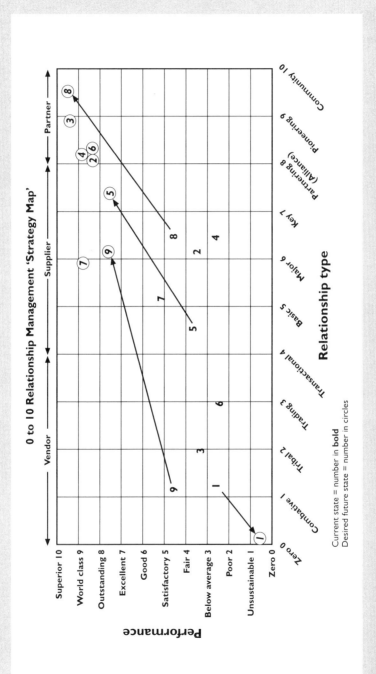

Fig. 3.3 *Analysis of the top nine relationships*

Why is a 'paradigm shift' important?

'You see things and you say why. I dream of things that never were and say why not.'

George Bernard Shaw

Paradigms are behaviours, practices, policies and rules that we take as given and that often go unchallenged. We assume them to be true and immutable. Paradigm shifts can be big or small but, nevertheless, they are all fundamentally important for those people practising the prevailing paradigm. They are not just about the world being round and not flat, or the earth revolving around the sun and not being the centre of the solar system, or being able to travel faster than the speed of sound.

A paradigm shift can be as simple as moving from an 'overtime' environment based on rework and breakdown to a fixed 'annualised salary' based on high productivity and reliability. Entering a two-way, open-book, performance-based, transparent and trusting relationship and not a closed-book, low-trust, non-transparent relationship is still a paradigm shift for many organisations. Co-location, people exchange and secondment across customers and suppliers, supplier management of customers' inventories, shared intellectual property, and early supplier involvement in the concept, design and strategy stages can also be paradigm shifts for many.

In all aspects of our lives changing a paradigm means fundamentally altering the way things are done. We measure our success by our ability to solve problems using the rules of the paradigm.[1]

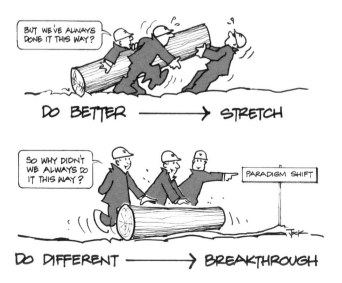

Listed in Table 3.5 is a checklist of 12 paradigm shifts for partnering relationships.

Table 3.5 *Paradigm shifts for partnering relationships*

Required paradigm	Is this paradigm operating—yes/no?
1.	No contract, no term relationship (evergreen) relationships or equivalent, based on performance, open-book practices and transparency
2.	Customer/supplier partner 'no blame' interdependence—all partners have something fundamental to gain and something fundamental to lose from the success or failure of the relationship (i.e. the relationship is based on win/win or lose/lose; the win/lose options have been eliminated)
3.	The mindset and operating philosophy that 'we are no longer interested in your margins (and squeezing them); we are now interested in your ideas and sharing the benefits of innovation'
4.	Getting paid on the quality of outputs, outcomes, performance and effect of products and services—not unit price or inputs (e.g. gain/pain share, risk/reward-based remuneration)
5.	No tender relationship—a tender process may be the mechanism by which the relationship starts, but the relationship is retained based on superior benchmarked performance based on agreed outcomes, KPIs and associated targets
6.	Co-supplier or 'complementor' relationships (e.g. clusters, networks, consortia) and joint benchmarking between co-suppliers
7.	A joint 'trust charter' detailing the mindsets, practices, behaviours and attitudes around what trust looks like for the relationship is agreed to and operating
8.	Joint partnering/alliance strategy, charter (i.e. vision, key objectives and guiding principles), and KPIs and targets in place and operating
9.	Joint succession plans for key influencers and partnering champions
10.	'Reverse negotiations' (i.e. partners negotiating on each other's behalf) or 'one team' negotiations (i.e. mutually agreed decisions based on shared information, for mutual benefit, take the place of traditional negotiating styles and techniques)
11.	Open access to previously hidden treasures, opportunities and best practices
12.	A move from 'supplier of choice' to 'relationship of choice' (i.e. one team, one direction, common goals)

Question 1: *Can you think of any other paradigm shifts that are needed for your partnering relationship to succeed?*

Question 2: *How many paradigm shifts do you have in place for your strategic partnership?*

As a guide, a genuine strategic partnership or alliance in the early stages of development will need three to four paradigm shifts operating. Robust, developed and well-performing partnerships will have up to six paradigm shifts operating. An outstanding, world-class partnership will have nine or more paradigm shifts being demonstrated.

SmartChem and SuperCat ... continued

SmartChem and SuperCat completed the checklist in Table 3.5 and scored 0 out of 12. They were embarrassed and dumbfounded. They thought they were doing better. The core team put forward a recommendation to work on three or four paradigm shifts as part of Horizon 1 and the others would follow later. The initial paradigms to be developed were numbers 2, 3, 7 and 8 from Table 3.5.

Trust in people, systems and processes

Trust is the foundation upon which a strategic partnership is built. Without trust, there can be no relationship. All the guiding principles for the relationship will be based on trust. There are three 'trust' questions you need to ask:

Question 1: *Is trust important for 'this' relationship? If yes, then go to question 2.*

Question 2: *If trust is important, define it. Stephen Covey[2] says 'trust is a function of competence as well as character'.*

Question 3: *Now for the details—What does trust look like specifically for the relationship under review? How does trust manifest itself in behaviours, attitudes, mindsets, policies and practices?*

Trust looks like no secrets, no lies and no unpleasant surprises

SmartChem and SuperCat ... continued

Trust is the basis upon which this relationship will be successful and mutually beneficial. Trust is a function of competence as well as character. Trust for the SmartChem and SuperCat relationship looks like the following attitudes, behaviours, mindsets, practices and performance levels:

- co-location
- joint teaming
- report by exception
- quality coming first
- value for money, and *not* the cheapest price
- proactive not reactive response to problems and issues
- progress payments and invoices paid in full and on time to agreed terms
- integrity—do what you said you were going to do
- agreeing targets, goals and milestones that are *SMART* and then sticking to them (SMART stands for: S = specific; M = measurable; A = achievable; R = relevant/realistic; and T = trackable)
- letting others know as early as possible and proactively when these targets, goals, milestones can't be reached
- a win/win, positive approach to resolving conflicts and problems
- open, honest, timely, accurate and relevant sharing of information and ideas
- our success is your success
- friendship and having respect for each other, no second guessing
- no 'person marking' and no shoulder watching
- no secrets, no lies and no unpleasant surprises
- common systems.

The moral versus legal agreement

Strategic partnering is often talked about as fundamentally a moral agreement and putting the 'handshake back into business'. It is about fair-minded and reasonable people, acting in good faith and focused on clear objectives for which they hold themselves mutually accountable. It is a performance-based, principle-centred, leadership-focused approach to relationship management. Good partnering and alliance agreements capture the spirit/intent of the relationship as well as the legally binding obligations.

Question 1: Is a moral agreement (e.g. the trust components) important to your business, as well as a legally binding contract?

Question 2: Which should you act on first—the moral or the legal agreement?

Question 3: *If the moral agreement is important and the first thing you act on, what is the moral agreement? Without it there is only the contract to fall back on.*

Supporting the partnering and alliance relationship

Successful strategic partnerships are often compared to successful fourth marriages. They are a triumph of hope over experience.

Question: *Are you bringing any baggage (perceptions, experiences, fears, prejudice) to the partnering table?*

SmartChem and SuperCat ... continued

SmartChem and SuperCat's agreement was very traditional, detailed, prescriptive and, from everyone's perspective, was one-sided. It included liquidated damages, unlimited liabilities, no incentive for innovation, and was built on combative yearly pricing reviews for the catalysts supplies, and a schedule of rates, fixed price, lump sum, market bid, tender-based arrangements for engineering services. This had to change and was one of the paradigm shifts to be implemented.

The distinguishing features of strategic partnering agreements include:

- They are plain language and positive documents.
- The spirit is one of 'fair dealing'.
- The guiding principles and intent are stated up-front.
- The leadership team is the ultimate review body.
- All roles and responsibilities are clearly defined.
- The team approach, shared financial motivation and common goals are clearly documented.
- Risk allocation is often linked to gain/pain remuneration to drive continuous and breakthrough improvement.
- There is a 'no blame', win/win approach to issues resolution.

Exercise: What are the characteristics of your relationships?

Business partnerships and alliances, spouse/partner relationships and best friend relationships have a lot in common. For your own relationships, list the characteristics of each. As a comparison, list the characteristics of the very worst relationship you have ever been involved with. When you have completed the table, think about any similarities between the relationships.

Partnerships and alliances are about people and change

Relationship management and partnering and alliancing are a process of managing change. There are broadly four types of people and their ability to adapt to change.

- ***Innovators.*** These are the partnering pioneers who drive the process from rough concept to practical application. They are the champions and leaders and have the courage, intuition and long-term perspective to make the vision a reality. They are critical to your partnering and alliance success.

- **Early adaptors.** The early adaptors are the first group of non-innovators to accept the change process. They question, challenge, modify and improve. Typical statements from early adaptors are: 'Wow, what a great idea. I wish I had thought of that' or 'Can I modify it and improve on it?'
- **Followers.** These people follow the lead from the other three types. In good organisations they are highly skilled, enthusiastic and committed individuals doing a good job. They are 'Prove it to me' people—their level of support and involvement in the process will be based on the quality of argument and delivery of results.
- **Terrorists.** Terrorists are those individuals who actively, overtly or covertly, oppose or deliberately undermine and 'white ant' the change process. They are the snipers, gatekeepers and filters of power and information. They will ignore the principle and reject the process. Manage them up as they can become great innovators, or manage them out (i.e. 'exit stage left'), or put them in a place where they can do no damage.

The journey of change

Innovators and terrorists share three qualities: they are all stubborn, passionate and unreasonable people. The innovators use those qualities constructively for mutual benefit, while the terrorists use the same qualities destructively for self-interest. Great satisfaction and benefit can be gained from turning a terrorist into an innovator.

Question 1: Who are your innovators, early adaptors, followers and terrorists?

Question 2: How are you identifying, developing, inspiring and challenging your innovators, early adaptors and followers? How are you managing and dealing with the terrorists?

SmartChem and SuperCat ... continued

Brian, Katherine and the core team identified people in all four categories and developed an action plan to encourage, develop or rectify.

The partnering development curve—partners in time

> *'Partnerships and alliances are a process not an event, a journey not a destination. They take time.'*

Partnerships and alliances take time and go through different phases and often start out of a crisis or an impending crisis, as shown on the partnering development curve (see Fig. 3.4). It is the crisis that often provides the catalyst and incentive for change.

Question 1: *What is your burning platform for change?*

Question 2: *Where are your relationships positioned on the partnering development curve?*

SmartChem and SuperCat ... continued

There was no doubt, after 10 years of inconsistent performance, variation and instability in the relationship that a crisis point had been reached. There was no bridging here (i.e. the dotted line on Fig. 3.4). All on the core team acknowledged they had a crisis, which could be used as a 'catalyst' for essential change. They agreed that part of the first horizon was building trust, credibility and keeping commitments by doing what all parties said they would do.

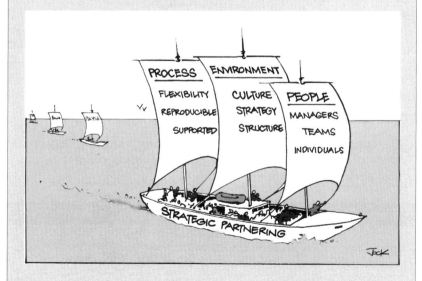

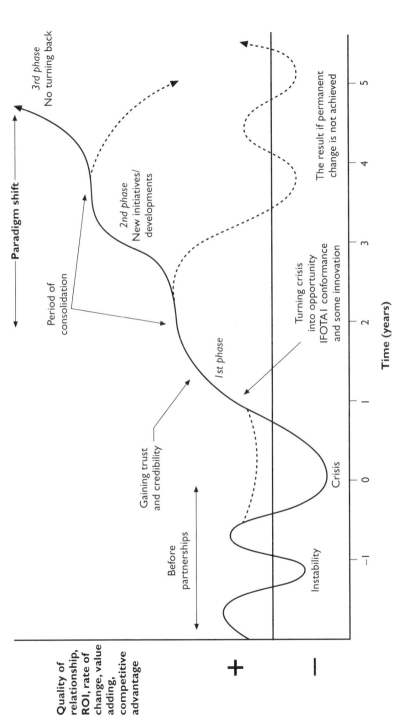

Fig. 3.4 *The partnering development curve*

Chapter 4

Culture—the relationship principles and values

What is culture?

Corporate culture is all about 'the way we do things around here'. It is the deep-rooted values, beliefs and underlying assumptions of an organisation that determine how it functions and how it interacts with both its internal and external environment. It is what causes people to think the way they do, say the things they say and do the things they do when involved with the organisation and its customers and suppliers. Partnering and alliance cultures are principle-centred, leadership-focused, innovation-driven, empowering, responsive and highly adaptive to change.

Every organisation has a culture—good, bad or indifferent. Strategic partnering and alliancing requires effective cross-fertilisation of people skills, functions, departments, customers, suppliers, ideas and innovation. It therefore requires particular cultural qualities and characteristics. Understanding your culture and having cultural alignment between your organisation and your partner organisation/s will generate a more enjoyable, productive and rewarding relationship.

Question 1: Does your organisation have what it takes to be an outstanding, best practice business partner?

Question 2: Is your organisation culturally equipped for partnerships and alliances?

Exercise: A quiz on your culture[1]

Rate your organisation (or a specific relationship) on a scale of 1 to 10, with 1 being your organisation is most like the picture on the left and 10 being your organisation is most like the picture on the right.

1. **Autonomy**—the ability of individuals to exercise initiative in their jobs

1 – 2 – 3 – 4 – 5 – 6 – 7 – 8 – 9 – 10

2. **Control**—the nature of coordination procedures used and the leadership characteristics displayed in the organisation

1 – 2 – 3 – 4 – 5 – 6 – 7 – 8 – 9 – 10

3. **Recognition and reward for performance**—the behaviours that are valued and rewarded in the organisation

1 – 2 – 3 – 4 – 5 – 6 – 7 – 8 – 9 – 10

4. Change tolerance—the willingness and capability of the organisation to change

1 – 2 – 3 – 4 – 5 – 6 – 7 – 8 – 9 – 10

WE ARE RESTRICTED, NARROW MINDED AND RESIST CHANGE

WE ARE FAST, FLEXIBLE AND RESPONSIVE TO CHANGE

5. Conflict tolerance—the way in which conflict arises and how it is managed

1 – 2 – 3 – 4 – 5 – 6 – 7 – 8 – 9 – 10

BLAME, FINGER POINTING, DENIAL, CONFRONTATION

PROACTIVE PROBLEM SOLVING AND JOINT RESOLUTION OF ISSUES

6. External coping—the way in which the organisation understands and responds to its external environment

1 – 2 – 3 – 4 – 5 – 6 – 7 – 8 – 9 – 10

FORTRESS MENTALITY, DEFENSIVE, PROTECTIVE, RESISTING CHANGE, APATHETIC, FEARFUL

ONE TEAM, ONE DIRECTION, COMMON GOALS, OUTWARD FOCUSED

7. Internal organising—the nature of collaboration and cooperation within the organisation

1 – 2 – 3 – 4 – 5 – 6 – 7 – 8 – 9 – 10

DISORGANISED, INDIVIDUAL FOCUS, NO TEAMWORK OR COMMON GOALS

ONE COHESIVE TEAM ACROSS DEPARTMENTS AND FUNCTIONS

8. Identity—the way in which employees identify with the organisation

1 – 2 – 3 – 4 – 5 – 6 – 7 – 8 – 9 – 10

SHAME AND INDIFFERENCE

PRIDE, PASSION AND COMMITMENT

9. Communication—the pattern and extent of information exchange within the organisation

1 – 2 – 3 – 4 – 5 – 6 – 7 – 8 – 9 – 10

FRUSTRATING PAPER TRAILS, ENDLESS MEMOS AND COVERING YOUR BACKSIDE

OPEN, HONEST, TIMELY, ACCURATE, RELEVANT COMMUNICATION AND INFORMATION SHARING

10. **Legacy focus**—the way in which the organisation relates to broader social, business and environmental issues, and activities beyond its immediate business boundaries

1 – 2 – 3 – 4 – 5 – 6 – 7 – 8 – 9 – 10

INWARD NARROW FOCUS

TRIPLE-BOTTOM-LINE FOCUS AND WIDER RESPONSIBILITIES CONSIDERED

Total score out of 100 =

Rating: If your score is greater than 80/100 and you scored greater than 7/10 in every category, you are in good shape for high-performance partnering. If your score is between 50/100 and 80/100 and you scored greater than 5/10 in every category, you are in the supplier segment at varying performance levels or high-performing vendor relationships. If your score is less than 50/100, you are more comfortable with vendor relationship approaches.

Culture and leadership

> 'There is a difference between leadership and management. Leadership is of the spirit, compounded of personality, vision and training. Its practice is an art. Management is a science and of the mind. Managers are necessary, while leaders are indispensable.'
>
> Admiral J. Moorer, US Navy

There are five key roles for 'leaders' in strategic partnering relationships:

1. to set a world class and achievable vision, a broad strategy and standards for partnerships and alliances with a long-term focus that inspires all in the organisation
2. to lead and coach others in creating a learning environment based on continuously improving skills and competencies, on the delivery of superior performance, and on trust—an environment where individuals and teams

are encouraged to perform, are empowered and are committed to their full potential

3. to suitably reward and recognise high performance and outstanding achievement in skills development, innovation and leadership, whether individual or team-based

4. to create an environment where people enjoy coming to work: a place where they are challenged by the expectations and the opportunities; where calculated and educated risk taking is encouraged and honourable, while courageous and intelligent failure is accepted; where barriers and obstacles to effective communication and performance have been removed

5. to support and actively participate in the partnering and alliance process and relationship development.

Partnerships and alliances involve strong, inspirational and visionary leaders, with high levels of personal drive, competence and integrity.

Question: *Why would anyone want to be led by you?*

Chapter 5

Strategy—the relationship business drivers and value propositions

What is strategy?

Strategy positions the business in how it relates to its external environment, usually within a three-year to five-year timeframe. Strategic partnerships and alliances cannot exist in isolation. They are a fundamental part of your organisation's strategy, and will play an important role in the execution of your organisation's strategy. Your organisation's and your partner's strategies need to support an effective partnering and alliance approach. Extend this process up and down the supply chain and you will develop an integrated set of partner organisations all pursuing effective and synergistic strategies based on delivering superior products and services. This will generate profitable growth and/or sustainable competitive advantage for customer and supplier partners.

Good partners manage strategy and complexity together

'In the race of life always bet on self-interest.[1] The challenge for good partners is to align self-interest with mutual benefit.'

A variety of factors will influence the strategy for your partnership, including your organisation's and your partner organisation's:

- business drivers
- value propositions
- core competencies.

Business drivers

Business drivers are the goals and underlying assumptions that provide the organisation with the platform, the direction and the motivation to develop and execute its strategies. Your business drivers need to be aligned with your partner's business drivers.

Exercise: Are your business drivers aligned?

To understand the degree of alignment between you and your partner, identify, in Table 5.1, those business drivers that complement each other and those that are in conflict with each other.

Table 5.1 *The degree of alignment*

Your business drivers	Joint/shared business drivers	Your partner's business drivers

After identifying your business drivers and their alignment with those of your partner organisation, you need to determine if your relationship reflects the qualities of a high-performance strategy.

Exercise: Does your relationship reflect a high-performance strategy?

Use the ten components of a high-performance strategy for strategic partnerships listed in Table 5.2 to rate your relationship out of 10 (0 = lowest score; 10 = highest score).

Table 5.2 *Rate your relationship*

Qualities of a high-performance strategy	Your partnership relationship score out of 10
1. High customer focus and supplier engagement—continuous and breakthrough improvement, early collaborative, transparent engagement and involvement in information sharing and long-term strategy development	
2. Principle based—integrity, reputation, brand building, trusting and trustworthy, doing what you said	
3. Compelling value propositions—opportunities beyond cheap price and low cost	
4. Value adding—delivered products and services positively impact market share, margin, price premiums, additional volumes, product/service development cycle times, level of differentiation	
5. Total cost reducing—total cost of ownership, removal of waste and duplication, lower operational costs	
6. Performance based—revenue and profits linked directly and indirectly to performance expectations, KPIs, measurement and remuneration	
7. Mutual-benefit focused—win/win, our success is linked directly to your success, joint strategy document between the partners, shared vision, common goals and mutually accountable KPIs	
8. World class or best practice standards and/or performance levels—benchmarked	
9. Innovation-driven—number and impact of new ideas, products and services	
10. Vehicle for internal transformation—best practice benchmarks and centres of excellence, learning and development	
Total out of 100 =	

Reality check: If you scored greater than 80 out of 100, or 8 out of 10 in all categories, you are in good shape.

SmartChem and SuperCat ... continued

SmartChem and SuperCat scored 24 out of 100 on their rating of the 10 components of a high-performance strategy, as shown in Table 5.3.

Table 5.3 *SmartChem and SuperCat's relationship score*

Qualities of a high-performance strategy	SmartChem and SuperCat's relationship score out of 10
1. High customer focus and supplier engagement	2
2. Principle based	3
3. Compelling value propositions	3
4. Value adding	4
5. Total cost reducing	3
6. Performance based	1
7. Mutual-benefit focused	2
8. World class or best practice standards and/or performance levels	3
9. Innovation-driven	2
10. Vehicle for internal transformation	1
Total out of 100 =	**24**

The current strategy did not support an effective partnering and alliance approach. Brian and Katherine decided to recommend a joint strategy development for senior management to review.

Value propositions

Value propositions go beyond the benefits to be gained from a focus on just price and cost. Value propositions are the value-added and/or other total cost benefits to be gained and the opportunities to be developed. The value propositions in strategic partnering and alliance relationships will reflect the opportunities and benefits to be gained for all the partners. They are the foundation of the relationship.

SmartChem and SuperCat ... continued

SmartChem and SuperCat came up with the following value propositions:

- easier and faster access and transition to new technologies
- the ability to leverage off or have access to partner's 'global' reach, capabilities, brand, market knowledge and networks
- removal of complexity and lower total operating costs
- improved speed to market for new products and services
- increased revenues, additional profits, increased margin through risk/reward-linked, performance-based remuneration
- greater integration, simplification and efficiency of operations
- improved brand and reputation
- significant improvement in risk management or significantly reduced or improved risk profile(s)
- significantly improved project delivery.

Question: What are the value propositions for your partnering relationship?

Core competencies

Core competencies[2] are those groups of activities, skills and technologies that a firm does well (ideally, world class) and which add direct value for the customer. In doing so, their competencies clearly advantage and differentiate the firm from its competitors, allowing the firm to extend itself into new markets, products and services. Understanding and developing core competencies is fundamental to any organisation striving for market leadership. Examples of core competencies are:

- Canon—precision engineering, fine optics, microelectronics and electronic engineering
- Honda—small engines and powertrains
- Sony—miniaturisation
- SKF (bearings)—antifriction and precision engineering
- Motorola—wireless communication
- Federal Express—logistics management.

Relationship management is a core competency for those organisations wanting to develop world class or best practice partnering and alliance relationships.

Question 1: What are your organisation's core competencies?

Question 2: What core competencies do you need to develop, acquire or leverage to fulfil your partner's, and your own, requirements and expectations?

> ### *SmartChem and SuperCat ... continued*
>
> SmartChem's core competencies are:
>
> - chemical solutions—products, services and innovation.
>
> SuperCat's core competencies are:
>
> - optimising chemical reactions
> - chemical reaction safety and containment
> - project management.

The key elements of a strategic partnership

The key elements of a strategic partnership are shown in Figure 5.1.

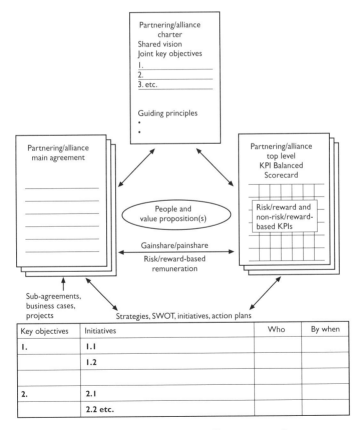

Fig. 5.1 *The key elements of partnering and alliance strategies*

What is the partnering charter?

The partnering charter is normally a single-page document detailing the shared vision, joint key objectives and guiding principles for the relationship. This simple document provides the visibility and the basis for measuring relationship performance. See Figure 7.1 (page 75) for the SmartChem and SuperCat charter.

Risk/reward-based remuneration

> '*You have to learn to love your partner's profit.*'
>
> Alistair Tompkin—Director of Power Generation, Hazelwood Power

Risk/reward-based remuneration adds the focus and the incentive to maximise mutual benefit from the shared vision and common goals of the partnering charter. As for loving your partner's profit, this is not just about tolerating or condoning profit but a genuine commitment to and desire for the supplier partner to earn better than expected profits based on better than expected outcomes delivered to the customer partner. 'Our success is your success.' Risk/reward-based remuneration itself is not a panacea, but when implemented well it is a very effective tool for aligning goals, behaviours, attitudes, mindsets and performance outcomes.

All customer/supplier relationships have profit at risk. The real issue is the level of openness, fairness and transparency with which the risk and the reward details are communicated and managed, as well as the business drivers and personal intent of the individuals involved.

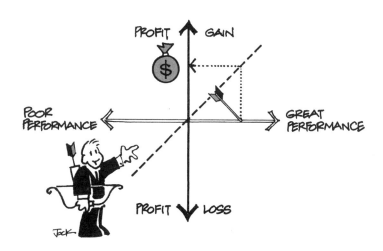

Risk/reward-based remuneration provides the key link between performance, measurement, behaviour/attitude, risk management and remuneration. The partners have something significant to gain from better than expected performance results and something significant to lose from worse than expected results. This is performance based on agreed desired outcomes and on a 'balanced scorecard' or 'performance scorecard' of risk/reward and non-risk/reward-based key performance indicators (KPIs). The balanced or performance scorecard details the hard and soft, leading and lagging KPIs, the performance targets that are associated with each of the joint key objectives on the charter and the expected profit levels that can be achieved. You can't manage what you can't measure, so you need a KPI scorecard.

In short the supplier's financial remuneration and financial success, often represented as profit, is linked directly to the customer's own success in the marketplace, as well as the performance and/or effect of the products and services delivered within the relationship. The supplier partner is therefore rewarded on the quality of the solutions and benefits generated, not on the cost or features of the purchased technology, products or services. The supplier partner gets paid on the quality of outputs and outcomes, not on the cost of inputs. The percentage of agreed profit and/or revenue, gain or loss, above and below the agreed target, is based on the overperformance or underperformance against agreed KPI targets.

This sharing of risk/reward also provides comfort to other stakeholder groups within or external to the partner organisations that the strategic partnering relationship is demonstrably delivering best value for money. When done well and for the right reasons, a risk/reward-based remuneration model is one of the most important aspects in ensuring and demonstrating the success and sustainability of the partnering relationship and the delivery of the associated value propositions. See the fourth edition of *The Strategic Partnering Handbook* for a full explanation and worked example of a risk/reward model with KPI scorecards.

Strategic partners concluding a risk/reward negotiation

SmartChem and SuperCat ... continued

Brian and Katherine led a small team to develop a risk/reward-based remuneration model, based on performance against agreed KPIs, which they developed from the joint key objectives in their partnering charter and the associated scorecard.

Focus on total value, not price

'Any idiot can reduce a price by 10 per cent to become more competitive, but if you can offer an electric power transmission cable under the Baltic one year earlier than your competition, that is of tremendous value to the customer, and your competitor can't touch you.'

Percy Barnevik, former Chairman of Asea Brown Boveri

The value question: *What value is this relationship delivering for my organisation over the alternatives? Can you answer this question at any time to the required detail?*

SmartChem and SuperCat ... continued

About the only things that SuperCat had were a key account management plan, which was not complete and was not shared with SmartChem, and a one-sided, prescriptive contract in favour of SmartChem. The rest of the components would need to be completed as part of Horizon 1. They also decided to take a different approach from their traditional negotiation techniques in that it would be a one-team approach, and not the adversarial, protective practices of the past.

Negotiating in a strategic partnership

Negotiating in a partnering environment is very different from the traditional deal-based, often drawn-out adversarial, win/lose, 'them and us' contests. Table 5.4 lists some of the characteristics of traditional negotiating versus partnering/alliance negotiating.

Partnering and alliance negotiations are approached in the same way as a good team would solve a problem or commercialise a good idea or innovation. They share lots of information, have clear objectives, think and behave win/win, have trust in each other, are open, honest and transparent, and work it through together around the table.

Table 5.4 *Approaches to negotiating*[3]

Traditional (contest) model	Partnering/alliance model
'Them and us' approach	One team, one direction, one set of goals approach
Short-term commitments	Long-term commitments and patience
Independent organisational goals/objectives	Shared vision and common goals
Safety (and less trust) in many suppliers	Trust in a single or few supplier partners
Little supplier contact with other suppliers	Partner may manage second tier suppliers
No joint benchmarking	Joint benchmarking for best practice and best value
Just-in-case inventory management	Just-in-time or supplier managed inventory
Adversarial/defensive negotiations common	Win/win, joint problem-solving approach
Competitive bid, often tender based, closed book	Open-book costing (two way) and transparency
Arm's length relationship	Supplier an extension of the customer's process
Lowest price/ambit claims	Best total cost and value
Departmental focus	Systems focus
Speeding up process steps	Eliminating and/or re-engineering
Suppliers push sales	Customer driven (i.e. pulls requirements)
Manufacturers define needs	Customers' needs define requirements
Specialisation	Highly integrated solutions
Information used for power	Information used for continuous and breakthrough improvement

TRADITIONAL NEGOTIATING

PARTNERING/ALLIANCE NEGOTIATING

Good partners eliminate the win/lose options. There are only two alternatives remaining: either win/win together or lose/lose together.

Good partners eliminate the win/lose options—
they're not always what they seem

Chapter 6

Structure—the relationship interface

Strategy determines your structure. Partnering/alliance structures, or the relationship interfaces between partners, that support the world class, best practice strategies will be team-based, multilevel, cross-organisational and cross-functional. Often co-located at the management and operations levels, these teams will be based on multilevel contacts and interfaces throughout the partner organisations, with open communications and high levels of trust and transparency.

Team members will have complementary skills and be committed to a shared vision, common goals, performance targets and a relationship approach for which they hold themselves mutually accountable.[1] Team members will be chosen on the basis of what is best for the relationship, irrespective of which company they work for. These external interfaces are supported internally by flat, flexible, team-based structures that are very adaptable to change.

A typical strategic partnering structure includes:

- a 'joint leadership team' (JLT), which is normally a small group (e.g. 2–6, depending on the size and nature of the relationship) of senior executives and managers from the partner organisations who represent the final review, leadership and management body for the relationship
- a 'joint management/operational team' (JMT), which has responsibility for the day-to-day, week-to-week operation of the relationship, and is accountable to the JLT for the effective delivery of the partnering charter vision and strategic objectives.

Figure 6.1 shows a typical strategic partnering/alliance structure.

SmartChem and SuperCat ... continued

SmartChem and SuperCat developed a structure based on the JLT/JMT approach. The JLT had four members: two people from SmartChem (Bob and the Chief Financial Officer) and two people from SuperCat (the Marketing Director and the Engineering Services General Manager). The JMT had eight members, again with 50:50 representation. Brian and Katherine were joint team leaders of the JMT and also participated on the JLT. The JLT met quarterly and the JMT monthly. They agreed that the roles and responsibilities of the JLT and JMT were as follows:

JLT roles and responsibilities

Approving

- appointment and/or removal of JMT members
- changes to the partnering charter and agreement
- the partnering strategy prepared by the JMT
- capital expenditure within authority levels
- senior level secondments, people exchanges, succession plans and significant resource/restructuring initiatives
- recommended variations to the remuneration model
- the partnering relationship's annual business plans and budget
- individual business cases or projects as appropriate
- strategies or initiatives that have been developed by the JMT
- any changes to the KPI scorecards recommended by the JMT
- performance-based remuneration outcomes that have been recommended by the JMT
- the risk management plans as recommended by the JMT.

Ensuring

- effective governance structures and policies for the relationship are in place
- remuneration incentives for the JMT are established

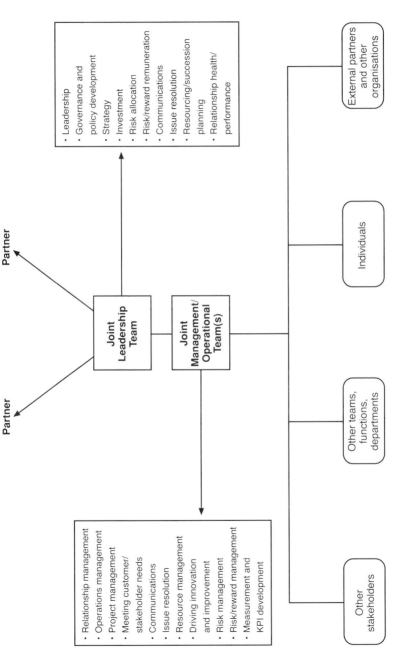

Fig. 6.1 *A typical strategic partnering/alliance team-based structure*

- the JMT is empowered and supported
- the partnering principles are satisfied in all respects
- the obligations and commitments of the relationship participants are fulfilled
- as a team, they set the example for partnering behaviour
- the ongoing corporate and management support for the partnering approach
- an environment that encourages honest, open, transparent and timely sharing of information.

Periodically reviewing

- the overall relationship 'health'/performance as measured by the KPI scorecards and outcomes from partnering survey(s)
- the achievement of specific business case or project-based KPIs
- the performance of the JMT against plan/strategy
- the strategic direction and other investment options for the relationship.

As well as

- being the ultimate review body for issue resolution within the relationship
- communicating the views, vision, strategic objectives, value propositions and performance outcomes of the relationship to the individual partner organisations, other stakeholders and third parties
- being an advocate for and representing the best interests of the partnering relationship
- managing the interpartner and intrapartner relationships
- where appropriate, acting as coaches, sponsors and mentors for other personnel in the relationship
- facilitating meetings and contacts internal and external to the partner organisations that will have a positive influence on the relationship.

JMT roles and responsibilities

- relationship management and leadership on a day-to-day basis at the operational level
- meeting and where appropriate exceeding customer requirements and stakeholder expectations
- being responsible for the cultural, strategy, structure, process/systems and people development and alignment for the partnering relationship
- ensuring there is an environment established that encourages honest, open communication and transparent, timely sharing of information
- implementing the directions and decisions of the JLT
- establishing the partnering relationship's business plans and associated strategies
- translating high-level strategies into operational plans

- delivering or realising the partnering charter key objectives as measured by the performance against the jointly agreed KPIs and associated targets on the relationship KPI scorecards
- monitoring the health of the relationship via relationship surveys and other means
- driving and inspiring innovation, new ideas and improvement opportunities at all levels of the relationship
- effectively managing the transition plan(s)
- developing and/or approving business cases and project scopes for submission to the JLT
- making recommendations or submissions for approval to the JLT on:
  - modifications to the relationship scope and/or associated agreements
  - personnel changes, secondments, people exchange programs, succession plans
  - remuneration levels (personnel and business/relationship performance)
  - business cases and associated projects
  - business plans/strategies
  - modifications to the partnering charter and KPI scorecards
  - unresolved issues or disputes
- identifying and/or initiating improvement opportunities or corrective actions to enhance performance
- ensuring personal and relationship key objectives are aligned
- ensuring the partner organisation business drivers are aligned with the partnering vision and key objectives as expressed in the partnering charter
- playing a key role in the proactive solving of problems and the joint resolution of issues via the issue resolution process
- coaching and mentoring others in partnering principles, concepts and practices
- managing important internal relationships and third party relationships
- effective resource allocation
- effective management of risk and risk allocation
- managing the risk/reward remuneration for the relationship and performance measurement associated with the over/under performance against agreed KPI targets
- setting up and managing effective lines of communication and communication protocols for the relationship
- recruiting people with the right attitudes and skills to support the relationship goals and key objectives
- reporting to the JLT at agreed and regular intervals on the:
  - performance of the relationship
  - opportunities for improvement
  - outstanding issues.

Exercise: Is your structure ready for this relationship?

Try this 10-question survey on your organisation's structure (see Table 6.1) to determine its suitability for a partnering relationship.

Table 6.1 *Survey on your organisation's structure*

Characteristic	Rating scale	Characteristic
1. Effectively, there is a single point of contact between customer and supplier (e.g. purchasing and sales) with both sides (from an internal and external perspective) protective of their positions and knowledge	1 2 3 4 5 6 7 8 9 10	1. An advanced or extensive multilevel contact structure exists between the customer and supplier with many people from many levels within and between the customer/supplier organisations having regular, open contact with each other
2. There is no formal team structure for managing this relationship	1 2 3 4 5 6 7 8 9 10	2. Cross-organisational partnering leadership and management teams or similar manage and coordinate the activities and developments between customer and supplier
3. Many functional, departmental, physical and other barriers exist that impede effective communication and business development between customer and supplier	1 2 3 4 5 6 7 8 9 10	3. Customers and suppliers exist in a seamless environment in this relationship where there are no barriers or demarcations to effective communication and business development
4. Power and influence is held by only a few individuals in our organisation	1 2 3 4 5 6 7 8 9 10	4. Power and influence for a few has been replaced by responsibility for many in our organisation
5. The organisation/relationship is hierarchical, with many layers	1 2 3 4 5 6 7 8 9 10	5. Effectively no layers exist within the organisation/relationship: it is a flat structure
6. Team membership never crosses functions or departments	1 2 3 4 5 6 7 8 9 10	6. In our organisation team membership often involves people from various functions and departments
7. Team membership never includes external customers' and suppliers' service providers	1 2 3 4 5 6 7 8 9 10	7. Team membership often includes external customers' and suppliers' service providers
8. Confrontation/tribalism/ rivalry is high between functions and departments	1 2 3 4 5 6 7 8 9 10	8. Confrontation/tribalism/rivalry do not exist between functions and departments
9. Communication is poor due to mistrust and often filtered or misleading information	1 2 3 4 5 6 7 8 9 10	9. Communication is open and based on trust and shared information (internally and externally)
10. In our organisation it is the structure of the organisation that determines the strategy that it deploys to the external marketplace	1 2 3 4 5 6 7 8 9 10	10. In our organisation it is the strategy that determines the supporting structure
Your total score out of 100 =		

Rate your organisation (or a specific relationship) on a scale of 1 to 10, with 1 being your organisation/relationship is more like the statement on the left and 10 more like the statement on the right of Table 6.1.

Rating: If you scored greater than 80/100 in total and greater than 7/10 for each category, you are in good shape for a high-performance partnering relationship. If you scored between 50/100 and 80/100 in total and greater than 5/10 for each category, this puts you in the supplier segment at varying performance levels or a high-performing vendor segment. If you scored less than 50/100, you are more comfortable with vendor relationship approaches.

Chapter 7

Process—the relationship roadmap

> 'Strategic partnering is a process, not an event; it is a journey, not a destination.'

The strategic partnering process is the basis on which customer and supplier partners are chosen and the relationship developed, managed and improved upon. The process should provide guidelines that enable people to think 'outside the square' as opposed to rigid 'belts and braces' procedures that so often confine or force people to think conventionally.

The 12 process motivators

The 12 motivators are the driving forces behind the process. They provide the reasons and the motivation to propel the partnership continually forward. As the partnership moves forward, the process will be motivated by the question: Will the next step …

1. add value
2. reduce costs
3. improve communication
4. develop trust
5. resolve conflicts
6. remove hidden agendas
7. provide leadership
8. empower people
9. gain commitment
10. develop ownership
11. break down departmental barriers
12. remove fear?

The 12 process steps

The 12 process steps provide the vehicle and structure by which the 12 motivators, as the drivers of the process, can be realised. They are the 'roadmap'. The 12 process steps are:

- select a partner
- review internal relationships (determining the willingness and capability to partner)
- review process progress with the partner and sharing information

- complete a requirements analysis (present and future)
- meet or exceed requirements 'In Full On Time to A1 specification' (IFOTA1)
- select leadership and management team members and review team performance
- conduct site visits
- review and develop customer/supplier partner skills requirements
- review supplier relationships upstream
- assess current and future technology requirements
- review interpartner and intrapartner networks
- develop/implement/review relationship strategy/action plan.

The outcomes of these steps are:

1. return on investment financial success
2. customer satisfaction
3. sustainable competitive advantage
4. world class/best practice
5. innovation
6. attitude.

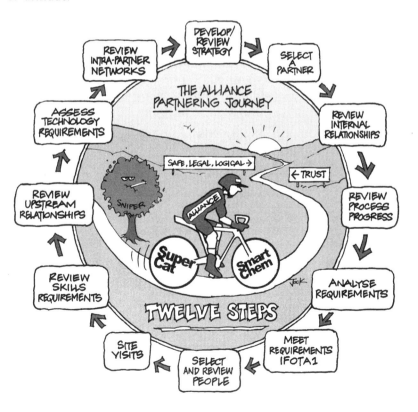

The 'roadmap' operating rules

The process 'roadmap' has three operating rules:

1. The steps are deliberately not numbered. Start where you want, with the choice or sequence of steps to be followed being infinitely flexible. It should be based on 'what is required to be done' and 'what is appropriate to the partner organisation(s) and the operating environment'.
2. More than one step can, will and should be worked on at any one time.
3. As long as the relationship exists there is no end; it is a continuous process.

For a detailed explanation of the process motivators, steps and outcomes, together with practical tools and worked examples, refer to *The Strategic Partnering Handbook*, fourth edition.

SmartChem and SuperCat ... *continued*

The checklist in Table 7.1 is what SmartChem and SuperCat concluded from their relationship analysis and detailed 12-step process review. For completeness Brian and Katherine thought it a good idea to initially review all the steps. Actions were then prioritised, accountabilities allocated and timelines agreed to.

The two partners found that it was the structured and creative implementation of the process steps that enabled them to move forward. The 12-step process helped them identify many things that had not been done before or even been considered. The three-horizon approach was then easily managed and implemented.

Question: *For each of the 12 steps in Table 7.1, how do you measure up?*

Table 7.1 *SmartChem and SuperCat's checklist for the 12 process steps*

Step: select a partner

Key points/actions	Done[1]	Impact[2]
1. Agree on the relationship scope and document the value propositions		
2. Confirm alignment of scope and value propositions with broader corporate/organisation strategy		
3. Complete a SWOT (Strengths, Weaknesses, Opportunities, Threats) and risk analysis for the relationship strategy to be deployed		
4. Review the impact the partnership will have on existing and future markets, customer and supplier relationships		

Notes: [1] Done—yes, no or N/A   [2] Impact/urgency—low, medium or high

Key points/actions	Done[1]	Impact[2]
5. Internal value chain and external supply chain understood and mapped		
6. Evaluate and select your customer/supplier partner(s) based on: • the strategic value they bring to the value propositions • the commercial value they bring to the value propositions • their willingness to partner • their capability to partner		
7. Supporting vendor/supplier/partner relationships identified (internal and external) and requirements and their performance reviewed		
8. Selection process to be completed by a team being a cross-section of people, skills, functions, influence with shared understanding and commitment (Note: Although an option, SmartChem and SuperCat did not take the business to the marketplace, but did this exercise jointly and openly with SuperCat using available benchmark data.)		
9. Competitor strategies understood and contingency plans developed		

Notes: [1] Done—yes, no or N/A   [2] Impact/urgency—low, medium or high

Step: review internal relationships (determining the willingness and capability to partner)

Key points/actions	Done[1]	Impact[2]
1. Internal communications and supporting relationships reviewed and action plans for improvement put in place		
2. Analysis of the organisation's (internal) willingness and capability to partner completed		
3. Internal trust developed and the attitudes, mindsets, behaviours and practices that make up that trust documented (e.g. via trust charter)		
4. Open, honest, accurate, transparent, timely, relevant communication and information sharing agreed and implemented		
5. Develop a high level of understanding of partnering/ alliance principles and practices (e.g. induction and other training programs)		
6. Individual and team roles/responsibilities for the alliance agreed and documented		
7. Work environment to be free from hidden agendas and internal conflict		
8. Develop internal partnering relationships where appropriate		
9. Internal innovators, champions and key influencers for the relationship identified and development plans put in place		

Notes: [1] Done—yes, no or N/A   [2] Impact/urgency—low, medium or high

Step: review process progress with the partner and sharing information

Key points/actions	Done[1]	Impact[2]
1. Conduct a partnering 'foundation' workshop and follow-up workshops with external facilitator and then follow up work group 'engagement' sessions at all levels to:		
— align strategy and confirm value propositions		
— develop common understanding of partnering principles and practice		
— develop a mutual trust between the partners		
— conduct a joint Strengths, Weaknesses, Opportunities, Threats (SWOT) analysis		
— develop the partnering charter detailing the shared vision, common goals (key objectives) and guiding principles for the partnership (see Fig. 7.1).		
— agree on scorecards of KPIs and targets for the relationship		
— agree on the governance approach, leadership and management team membership and individual roles/responsibilities		
— agree on the process for issue resolution/escalation		
— identify the opportunities for continuous and breakthrough improvement for the relationship		
— agree on information flows and communication protocols		
— identify opportunities to reduce waste and duplication.		
2. Open-book, transparent, risk/reward, gain/pain share remuneration model to be developed that links performance outcomes, measurement, remuneration and attitudes		
3. Conduct regular review workshops, 'toolbox meetings' and informal discussions at all levels between the partners to:		
— share information and build trust		
— report on progress/performance against objectives and external/internal benchmarks		
— review new opportunities for innovation, continuous and breakthrough improvement and profitable growth		
— challenge, inspire and lead the partnering change process		
— have fun and celebrate success		
4. Implement open, honest, accurate, transparent, timely, relevant communication and information sharing between the partners		

Notes: [1] Done—yes, no or N/A   [2] Impact/urgency—low, medium or high

Step: review process progress with the partner and sharing information (cont.)

Key points/actions	Done[1]	Impact[2]
5. Set up a joint benchmarking team, process and framework to enable ongoing, demonstrable and positive response to the 'value question'		
6. Set up a benchmark forum with selected customers and suppliers to share information and develop best practices		
7. Develop induction program(s) for educating new entrants to partnering		
8. Conduct formal and informal discussions on relationship performance and future direction with stakeholders and other key influencers		
9. Ensure the operating levels who have to make the relationship work are informed, involved and committed through ongoing communication, feedback and formal, regular workshops		
10. Relationship Alignment Diagnostic (RAD) analyses or relationship 'health checks' and/or surveys to be conducted on a regular basis		

Notes: [1] Done—yes, no or N/A   [2] Impact/urgency—low, medium or high

Shared vision: Role model partners making a difference by delivering best practice outcomes and valued solutions through spirited teamwork.

Joint key objectives
1. Zero harm to people, plant and environment.
2. Deliver products and services that meet or exceed customers requirements.
3. Achieve sound commercial outcomes for the partners.
4. Innovate for continuous and breakthrough improvement.
5. Build and maintain honest, open and timely communication and information sharing.
6. Promote the relationship to achieve broader business and legacy outcomes.

Guiding principles
• Act in a way that is best for the business and is safe, legal and logical.
• Do what you say—no unpleasant surprises.
• Trust, integrity, probity and professionalism.
• Proactive problem solving and joint resolution of issues.
• Be fair and reasonable.
• Commit to a 'no blame', high accountability culture.
• Have fun and celebrate success.

Fig. 7.1 *SmartChem and SuperCat's Strategic Alliance Partnering Charter*

Step: complete a requirements analysis

Key points/actions	Done[1]	Impact[2]
1. Customer and supplier partner requirements (current and future) jointly agreed, documented and shared with all involved with their delivery. Listen, question and challenge		
2. Match requirements (current and future) to internal specifications and willingness and capability to deliver		
3. Work process flows analysed for improvement and re-engineering opportunities		
4. Requirements regularly reviewed and benchmarked against world's best or industry best practice		
5. Stretch and breakthrough targets in scorecard format to be set against delivery of requirements to drive innovation and improvement		

Notes: [1] Done—yes, no or N/A   [2] Impact/urgency—low, medium or high

Step: meet or exceed requirements 'In Full On Time to A1 specification' (IFOTA1)

Key points/actions	Done[1]	Impact[2]

The quick fix or temporary solution

1. Ensure current performance levels against jointly agreed requirements are known

2. Ensure quick fixes and short-term opportunities are identified and implemented, with the 'low hanging fruit' quick wins captured

3. Look for problems and crises that can be turned into opportunities quickly and cost effectively

4. The foundations for permanent solutions, future systems, procedural changes and process stability laid

5. One-hundred-day improvement plan developed and implemented (i.e. Horizon 1)

Quality longer term solutions

1. Medium to longer term improvement plans developed and implemented as/when required

2. Quality and other systems and communications protocols in place to meet or exceed current and future partner requirements

3. Incentive and recognition programs in place

4. Opportunities for achieving broader business outcomes, profitable growth and legacy opportunities are regularly reviewed and actioned where agreed and appropriate

Notes: [1] Done—yes, no or N/A   [2] Impact/urgency—low, medium or high

Step: select leadership and management team members and review team performance

Key points/actions	Done[1]	Impact[2]
1. The JLT and the JMT and supporting structure put in place with clear objectives and accountable KPIs		
2. Team member selection based on 'best person for the job', irrespective of the organisation worked for, skills required, cost incurred or location		
3. Team member roles and responsibilities clear, documented and communicated		
4. Appropriate empowerment and authority levels given		
5. Team sponsors in place		
6. Regular meeting schedule for relationship review and improvement implemented and open lines of communication activated		
7. Succession plans for team members and other key influencers developed		
8. Links and feedback mechanisms with other teams, functions, departments and business units identified and working effectively		
9. Relationship performance objectives and incentive and recognition programs in place		

Notes: [1] Done—yes, no or N/A   [2] Impact/urgency—low, medium or high

Step: conduct site visits

Key points/actions	Done[1]	Impact[2]
1. Site visits, internal and external with partner(s) occur regularly to:		
— meet the people		
— understand the culture		
— build ownership and commitment at all levels		
— share information		
— resolve issues		
— discuss opportunities for improvement		
— innovate and cross-fertilise ideas		
— build trust and develop friendships		
2. Third-party benchmark site visits take place regularly		
3. Guidelines for site visits developed and communicated		

Notes: [1] Done—yes, no or N/A   [2] Impact/urgency—low, medium or high

Step: review and develop customer/supplier partner skills requirements

Key points/actions	Done[1]	Impact[2]
1. Determine the skills required to meet current and future customer requirements and update on a regular basis		
2. Skills audit completed and updated regularly		
3. Skills gap identified		
4. Training and development programs implemented		
5. Joint partner training programs/initiatives in place		
6. People exchange programs and secondments to occur as appropriate		
7. Co-location of partners and other selected third parties as appropriate		
8. Formal links to educational institutions developed as appropriate		
9. Relationship management with specific focus on partnering being developed as a core competency for the organisation		
10. Internal and external relationship coaches used to develop key influencers, and partnering and alliance managers		

Notes: [1] Done—yes, no or N/A   [2] Impact/urgency—low, medium or high

WE'RE GOING TO NEED A DIFFERENT SET OF SKILLS IN THE FUTURE...

Step: review supplier relationships upstream

Key points/actions	Done[1]	Impact[2]
1. Important supplier relationships reviewed and current states and desired future states for the relationships identified and located on the 0 to 10 Relationship Management Matrix		
2. Supplier reduction program in place to integrate services, reduce variation and total cost of ownership, and improve quality and performance		
3. First-tier suppliers manage second-tier suppliers where appropriate		
4. Supplier performance objectives, KPIs and stretch targets in place and managed for improvement		
5. Co-location of suppliers (internal and external) as appropriate		
6. Performance, gain/pain share partnering relationships developed with selected suppliers		
7. Collaborative benchmarking process developed between suppliers to develop and share best practices for mutual benefit		
8. Innovation, continuous improvement and breakthrough thinking encouraged with top supplier group		
9. As appropriate, develop co-supplier relationships with competitors and/or product/service complementors to enhance competitive advantage and superior performance delivery to customers		
10. Regular reviews with top suppliers conducted for feedback and improvement		
11. Second-tier or sub-alliance partners identified and relationships developed		

Notes: [1] Done—yes, no or N/A   [2] Impact/urgency—low, medium or high

Step: assess current and future technology requirements

Key points/actions	Done[1]	Impact[2]
1. Technology gap analysis (current and future) completed and in alignment with each partner's business strategy, the relationship value propositions and customer requirements (current and future)		
2. Action plans and/or technology roadmap in place for improvement		
3. Process in place for regularly reviewing and benchmarking technology requirements		
4. Opportunities for technology integration, exchange explored and benefits identified		
5. Evaluation of technology acquisition, and licensing completed and actions in place as appropriate		
6. Opportunities for process, procedures and systems alignment/integration that support the relationship and improvement plans in place		

Notes: [1] Done—yes, no or N/A   [2] Impact/urgency—low, medium or high

Step: review interpartner and intrapartner networks

Key points/actions	Done[1]	Impact[2]
1. Interpartner and intrapartner relationship maps complete and opportunities for improvement in personal relationships, communications and service delivery identified		
2. Succession plans for key players/influencers in place		
3. A high level of open, transparent communication and information sharing exist and seamless relationships developed		
4. Partner 'coaches' identified and/or being developed		
5. Buy-in, support and commitment to be gained from all key influencers and major stakeholders		
6. Terrorists, followers, early adaptors and innovators of change known, and plans are in place to manage/improve		

Notes: [1] Done—yes, no or N/A   [2] Impact/urgency—low, medium or high

Step: develop/implement/review relationship strategy/action plan

Key points/actions	Done[1]	Impact[2]
1. Integrated partnering strategy in place (i.e. one team, one plan, one direction, common goals)		
2. Buy-in for the strategy gained from all key stakeholders		
3. Performance against the strategy objectives, initiatives, KPIs and agreed targets reviewed regularly by the JLT and JMT and communicated to all key stakeholders		
4. Strategy linked directly to relationship performance, innovation and improvement opportunities, risk management, KPI scorecards, gain/pain share remuneration and commercial arrangements, reward and recognition schemes, personal development and training activities		

Notes: [1] Done—yes, no or N/A   [2] Impact/urgency—low, medium or high

Chapter 8

People—the relationship delivery

None of these high-performing, collaborative and strategic relationships are successful without the right people, doing the right things, in the right way, for the right reasons. Delivery on the value propositions and shared goals is but a dream otherwise. So who are they—these partnering managers, champions, pioneers, 'passionate ones' and key influencers? Where are they from and what are their qualities/competencies?

The 'job description' for a partnering manager

An effective partnering or alliance manager requires specific skills. The purpose of their role is to lead and manage the overall wellbeing, continuous and breakthrough improvement of the strategic partnering relationship in the short, medium and long term.

Responsibilities

The responsibilities of a partnering or alliance manager include the following:

- to manage the complexity and networks of the alliance/partnership
- to be the partnering, operations management team leader with overall accountability and responsibility for the wellbeing of the relationship(s) in the short, medium and long term
- to be responsible for: financial performance; meeting or exceeding customer requirements; ensuring sustainable competitive advantage for the partners; identifying and implementing best practices and innovation opportunities; and ensuring the right attitudes, mindsets and behaviours are in place
- to be a member of the joint leadership team as appropriate
- to take a management and leadership role over people and teams who don't report directly
- to be responsible, with the joint leadership and management teams, for the development, implementation and delivery of short-, medium- and long-term strategies and key objectives for the partnership

- to provide periodic progress reporting to senior management
- to be a master trouble shooter and problem solver
- to be innovative and creative in developing technical and non-technical opportunities/solutions
- to maintain and develop internal and external relationships of importance to the partnership
- to work with and coach counterparts, other teams and individuals in partnering and alliancing for continuous improvement
- to be a persuader, influencer, coach and facilitator at all levels from senior management to the shop floor
- to develop and deliver against the partnering KPIs and targets
- to lead the process of setting performance stretch targets and identifying breakthrough opportunities
- to understand and improve partner organisational alignment with culture, strategy, structure, process and people
- to lead the development of new ideas, incentive programs, training and development programs
- to build trust, respect and credibility within and as appropriate external to the relationship and with key stakeholders
- to link the immediate partnering relationship to the 'bigger picture' and the achievement of longer term organisational and business goals, with social, environmental and broader legacy benefits
- to balance company and partnering relationship loyalties
- to be a 'champion of the cause' in taking strategic partnering and alliancing from rough concept to practical application
- to take calculated and educated risks for continuous and breakthrough improvements.

Skills requirements

The skills that a partnering or alliance manager needs include skills in the following areas:

- communications
- interpersonal relationships
- leadership and management
- coaching
- total quality
- specific technical skills as required
- strategic influencing
- strategic thinking
- innovation/creativity
- team leadership and team building
- conflict resolution

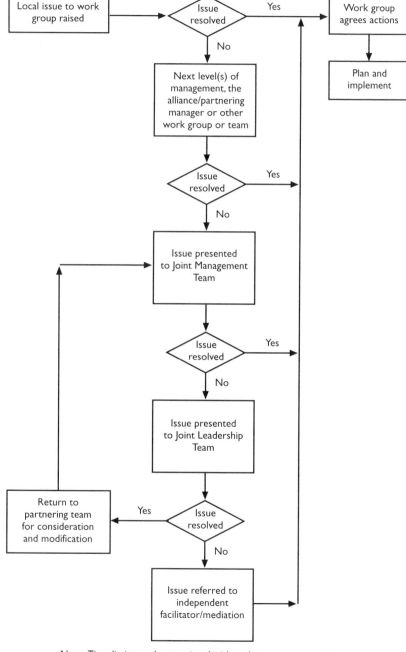

Note: Time limits can be associated with each step as appropriate

Fig. 8.1 *The issue resolution process (sample)*

- financial
- project management.

See the fourth edition of *The Strategic Partnering Handbook* for a full list of partnering and alliance manager competencies.

These same responsibilities and skills are, to varying degrees, applicable to partnering and alliance team members and others at the operating and management levels who are involved in the delivery of desired outcomes and relationship management, performance and improvement.

Issue resolution in partnering relationships: the ground rules

There are nine ground rules for resolving issues:

1. Resolve all issues within the partnering relationship.
2. Unresolved issues are to be escalated by both partners, in an agreed timely manner, before causing delays, cost increases or other negative effects.
3. Resolve issues at the lowest level.
4. Do not jump levels of authority.
5. Do not ignore the issue or allow a 'no' decision.
6. If appropriate, extend the decision time needed to reach agreement with the approval of a level above the point of indecision.
7. An issue can be escalated earlier than the process timeframe by mutual agreement.
8. Complete the feedback loop to the issue initiator.
9. No one has the right to 'screw up' the agreement or the relationship.

The process by which issues are resolved will vary. Figures 8.1 and 8.2 show two ways in which issues can be resolved.

Question: How does this issue resolution process apply to your relationship?

Level	Partner A	Maximum time to resolve or escalate	Partner B
1			
2			
3			
4			
5			
6			

Fig. 8.2 *The issue resolution/escalation process (sample)*

Who are the partnering 'champions'?

Partnering champions can be internal or external to your organisation. They are usually:

- young, capable, intelligent, principled and ambitious individuals on the way up
- older and experienced senior managers and leaders with the right experiences, skills and attitudes, and wanting to do something different
- experienced business people, specialists and professionals with the right attitudes and qualities who are challenged and excited by the new opportunity and career path
- innovators, space cadets, boundary riders, pioneers and tear-aways prepared to challenge prevailing paradigms, go beyond traditional limits, take calculated and educated risks and think 'outside the conventional square'.

Question: Do you have the right people, with the right skills, doing the right things, in the right way, for the right reasons?

Epilogue—A short story to end with

The journey continues…partnering workshop

It is two years since the original workshop that kicked off the partnering journey and where Brian had spoken the famous words: 'We must make a fundamental improvement in this relationship in both approach taken and performance achieved. Otherwise I think the relationship should be terminated as neither company is benefiting.' While regular workshops had been held, it was time for a major relationship review with all the key players and to celebrate the major milestones reached. Much had happened in two years. The workshop had four objectives. They were to:

1. review progress and performance to date
2. reward and recognise all those people who had made a positive contribution
3. discuss the opportunities and challenges for the future
4. have some fun and celebrate success.

Bob, now the CEO of SmartChem, gave the opening address. He began, 'It has been an amazing two-year journey—with hard work, which has been satisfying and rewarding. The whole team is to be congratulated on what has been achieved. Let me share with you some of the highlights:

- Our joint safety performance including subcontractors has improved by a factor of 10 over the last two years, and we have been incident free now for nine months. Our overall safety, health and environmental performance, induction, education and management systems are now widely regarded and acknowledged as best practice in the industry.
- The service levels based on IFOTA1 (In Full On Time to A1 specification) KPIs, including project performance, have risen from a low of 70 per cent to 99 per cent last quarter.
- Product development times have halved from 14 months to less than seven months, and are continuing to reduce. The product-development-to-successful-commercialisation ratio has gone from 10:1 to 10:8—a remarkable turnaround.
- Within 12 months 20 per cent of revenue will come from new products and services developed in the last two years.
- Maintenance costs have been reduced by 50 per cent.
- Based on the data compiled by the joint benchmarking team this relationship is delivering demonstrable 'best value for money' and a big 'yes' to the Value Question.
- The work that has been done via the partnering approach has made a significant contribution to SmartChem increasing its market share by 15 per cent and improving our profitability by 30 per cent over the two-year period. Our share price has increased by 25 per cent during the same period.
- Both companies have recently signed a new long-term, risk/reward, gain/pain share, performance-based strategic partnering agreement as a clear sign of a long-term commitment to the relationship.
- The relationship surveys completed every six months with wide participation from both organisations at all levels would indicate that many if not all of the past bad/poor practices, behaviours and attitudes have been eliminated. To support this there has been no unnecessary escalation of issues or problems to the Joint Leadership and Management Teams for over 12 months. From a personal perspective and from the people I see and talk to a genuine trust has now developed between the people. This is the real measure of success for me.
- We are now using the SmartChem/SuperCat partnering model with several new and existing customers and on a selected basis in the development of other new business opportunities.
- There is co-location of relevant personnel and team-based management structures in place.
- Joint planning and forecasting has reduced inventory costs by 30 per cent.
- Because of the SmartChem success and growth, the SuperCat business has grown by 25 per cent generating a win/win for both partners. The

SuperCat leadership team members also tell me that other significant business opportunities have been won and existing customer and supplier relationships consolidated.

- From another perspective, the improvement in the SmartChem and SuperCat relationship has had a significant and positive influence on the wider internal SmartChem relationships and the internal transformation process. This has been of enormous assistance and value to me personally.'

The workshop team was rightly impressed and proud of what they had achieved. While this information was already known and widely communicated it was great to hear the acknowledgment from the customer partner's senior executive.

Brian then spoke about the lessons learnt: 'I don't need to tell you it has been a tough two years. I would echo Bob's comments on performance and the contribution you personally and your teams have made. It has been quite a remarkable achievement. There have also been many lessons learnt as well. We haven't always got it right the first time and as part of the journey and in the spirit and practice of improvement we need to continually challenge ourselves and others to do better. I personally have learnt an enormous amount about linking good strategy to value propositions and effective relationship management.'

Brian then went on to list some other lessons learnt.

- 'We did not enlist, engage and inform enough people at the operating level, the people who make these partnerships and alliances work, early enough in the process. We also didn't engage the legal and financial folk early enough. They are often the traditional custodians of corporate rules and policies. This made the process more difficult than it needed to be in the early days. Good induction, continuous education and communication is the key.
- As everyone knows through the "bus of change model" we had to manage some roadblockers as part of the change process. This was not done well initially. We now understand that sometimes tough decisions have to be made sooner rather than later. One of our greatest achievements has been to turn some of the "terrorists" into genuine innovators.
- Some key people have moved on, and in some cases we had not planned for their succession. This slowed the improvement process down. Effective succession planning is the key.
- There is continual pressure to achieve quick results with a short-term dollar focus. The balance between the short, medium and long term needs to be managed effectively.

- Frankly we hadn't factored in the time it would take to build internal willingness and capability to be good partners. It takes time to build trust and develop the skills needed. You have to plan for the journey.'

Brian added, 'I am however particularly pleased that real and sustainable change has taken place. I know this from the people I talk to and results that I see and also from some of the comments that have come back on the relationship surveys from the "shop floor".' Brian read out some of them:

- 'We are now one team, sitting down working together.
- It's a lot more fun and an enjoyable place to work.
- There is very little stress in the job now.
- Why didn't we always do it this way?
- People are open and honest—no more BS.
- We feel safer.
- We trust each other. People do what they say.
- There are fewer issues and not as much back-stabbing.
- There is no more fighting and working against each other.'

He continued, 'Our success has been achieved through the effective alignment of culture, strategy, structure, process and people. We have developed a highly adaptive, open and empowering culture around a performance-driven, value-adding strategy, supported by a team-based, multilevel contact structure, a structured but flexible relationship management "roadmap" and a highly skilled, committed and motivated workforce. While this has been hard work, the paradox is that we are enjoying ourselves more than ever.'

Katherine then commented, 'It would be impossible to go back to the way we used to do business together. There is no turning back now. Both companies via the partnering approach are leaving a legacy for the future and this, in the long term, will be our greatest achievement. I believe there is the opportunity for us to be genuine pioneers in our marketplace. One of the next opportunities is to build a broader and more engaged strategic partnering community—an integrated supply chain of like-minded strategic partners, integrated products and services delivering unbeatable best value and supporting more broadly the society and environment we all live in. As one team moving in one direction, we can make a real difference and, in a small way, we are making our world a better place. That should be our legacy. Great, isn't it!'

As always, Katherine put the journey into perspective. There was still much to do and much to learn.

The workshop then got down to the details of discussing and discovering new opportunities and drafting the plan for the next horizon. But it was not all work and no play. They finished within half a day and the afternoon was spent learning to sail. You see, as it turns out, one of the maintenance team was an ex-Olympian sailor and he was going to teach the team some new skills. They would celebrate and have a whole lot of fun as well.

Keep the faith
Stay focused and
Enjoy the journey

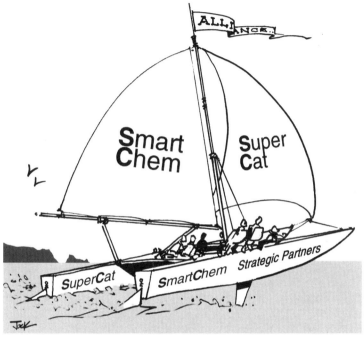

One team, one direction, common goals

The legacy effect

One hundred years from now
It will not matter
What kind of car I drove
What kind of house I lived in
How much money I had in my bank account
Nor what my clothes looked like
But one hundred years from now
The world will be a little better
Because I was important
In the life of a child

Author unknown (found under a fridge magnet)

Question: What are your relationships doing to leave a legacy and make our world a better place?

To get a relationship 'health check'

Go to **www.partneringcommunity.com** and complete the Relationship Alignment Diagnostic (RAD) based on the 0 to 10 Relationship Management Matrix.

Make our world a better place. When you have finished with this book, leave it in a place for others to read.

Endnotes

Chapter 2

1 Stephen Covey, *The Seven Habits of Highly Effective People*, Simon & Schuster, New York, 1990.

Chapter 3

1 Joel Barker, *Paradigm Pioneers*, 'Discovering the future series' (video), 1991.
2 Stephen Covey, presentation at the Sydney Opera House, May 1994.

Chapter 4

1 The first nine 'culture' headings in the quiz are taken from Gattorna Chorn, *Strategy Spotlight*, Vol. 2, November 1992, Gattorna Chorn Business Strategists.

Chapter 5

1 Attributed to Paul Keating, former Australian prime minister.
2 Gary Hamel and CK Prahalad, *Competing for the Future*, Harvard Business School Press, Boston, 1994, p. 223.
3 Based in part on the table presented by Ian Williams, Baxter Healthcare, at the 1994 National Purchasing and Materials Conference.

Chapter 6

1 Based on 'team' definition in Jon Katenback and Douglas Smith, 'The discipline of teams', *Harvard Business Review*, March–April 1993, p. 110.

Index